The post-war world

THE POST-WAR WORLD

a notebook review 1945–1965

by R. H. Thomas

LONDON

GEORGE PHILIP AND SON LIMITED

R. H. Thomas, M.A., is Headmaster
of The Grammar School, Fowey.

PRINTED IN GREAT BRITAIN

Preface

This notebook review of the years since the Second World War records the outstanding developments of the period and attempts to show their larger significance as factors in the overall growth of the present world situation.

One of the chief aims of the book is to help young people to understand the state of the world in which they live. This is a vital function of modern education, and in an age of increasing specialisation we neglect it at our peril.

I believe, too, that this recapitulation may also be of value to a wider public. It is dangerously easy to forget or ignore the past, even if we claim to have understood it. Indeed it seems to me that one of the weaknesses of democracy today lies in the separation of contemporary facts from their historical contexts. Many of us are content to believe that the truth can be reached if we discover the facts as they emerge in the contemporary world. I am convinced that this is not so, and that a real understanding of the origins of world problems can help towards wisdom and tolerance in our thinking.

R.H.T.

Contents

List of maps

1 The end of the Grand Alliance (i)

A *There was a growth of disunity between the British, Americans and Russians even before victory over Germany had finally been achieved:*

1 Russia's interpretation of the Yalta Agreement (February 1945) as regards the future Polish government and Poland's western frontiers:

a At Yalta the 'Big Three' agreed that the communist Polish (Lublin) administration, governing Poland behind the advance of the Red Army, should be 'reorganised on a broader democratic basis'. This was never carried out, and all attempts by Britain and the U.S.A. to insist on this clause were rejected in Moscow.

b Though neither Churchill nor Roosevelt would recognise the Oder–Neisse line as the western boundary for Poland, Stalin encouraged the Polish government to take over the administration of German territory east of these rivers. Moreover, the Red Army assisted the Polish government to expel seven million Germans who remained in the disputed territory.

2 Russia's ultimata to the Rumanian King Michael:

a February 27th, 1945. Mr Vishinsky (Mr Molotov's deputy in Bucharest) ordered the dismissal of General Radescu, leader of the Rumanian all-party government.

b March 3rd, 1945. Mr Vishinsky demanded the appointment of Petru Groza, leader of the Rumanian Communists, as Prime Minister.

3 The Berne negotiations:

a On March 10th, 1945, General Alexander reported that the German general, Karl Wolff, had agreed to open negotiations in Berne for the cessation of hostilities on the Italian front.

b When the Russians were informed, they accused Britain and the U.S.A. of 'carrying on negotiations . . . behind the back of the Soviet government' and in a later cable, Stalin accused Britain and the U.S.A. of making a separate peace with Germany.

B *The U.S.A. was unwilling to do anything that might antagonise Russia:*

1 For political reasons, Churchill wished to occupy Berlin before Zhukov and the Russians arrived. If this proved impossible, he wanted to occupy as much as possible of the east German grain area, in order to provide food for the industrial areas of west Germany when the war was over.

2 April 11th, 1945. The Americans reached the Elbe and secured a bridgehead across it. They were now only fifty-three miles from Berlin and Zhukov had not yet crossed the Oder, but neither Roosevelt nor Truman (after the former's death on April 12th) wished to deploy American troops for political purposes in Germany. Apart from advancing to the Baltic near Lübeck, the western Allies therefore halted on the Elbe to await the arrival of the Russians.

3 Roosevelt had, undoubtedly, put his faith in the United Nations Organisation, which was to be set up in San Francisco on April 25th. If the differences between Russia and the western Allies could be kept to a minimum until that date, he thought all would be well.

Some British people were amazed and indignant to learn that the U.S.A. was suspicious of their political ambitions in the post-war world, and they were quick to see in Franklin Roosevelt a naive innocence as far as European affairs were concerned. At Teheran in 1943, Stalin had been quick to spot the differences of opinion between the western leaders over the question of future allied strategy in the Mediterranean, and in February 1945, at Yalta, Churchill made it clear that though

Roosevelt might make allowances for Russian intransigence, as far as he was concerned the struggle for control of post-war Europe had begun.

There seems little doubt that these differences of outlook and approach between Roosevelt and Churchill stemmed from their differing historical backgrounds. Eleanor Roosevelt thought that 'the time that would be hardest for Churchill would be after the war', for, as she said, 'the world that had existed before the war had been a pleasant world as far as he was concerned, but could never be quite the same again'.

We shall never know whether Churchill would have been able to bring about the peaceful social revolution which occurred in Great Britain in the years after the war. Many people believe that the electorate showed great wisdom in overthrowing him in 1945, and that the policies advocated by his party at that time gave no indication that either he or they were aware of the new spirit that was abroad. This may or may not be true, but no one can deny that Churchill appreciated the dangers of aggressive Communism sweeping through Europe quicker than Roosevelt did. This is not however surprising when one realises that the U.S.A. had only entered the European lists in the twentieth century, and then only spasmodically.

It was at Algeciras, in 1906, that Franklin Roosevelt's swashbuckling ancestor, Theodore Roosevelt, first brought American pressure to bear in European politics, but it did not last. Though the U.S.A. eventually joined the Allies in the First World War, the failure of President Wilson to win Congressional support for the fourteen points of the Covenant of the League of Nations was only symptomatic of the U.S.A's contempt for the secret diplomacy of the old world, and of her desire to withdraw into her traditional isolationism.

Much of Wilson's idealism and some of the U.S.A's mistrust of European imperialism can be seen in the personality of

Roosevelt. If he trusted Russia more than Churchill did, it was because the U.S.A. and Russia seemed to have so much in common. They were both republics; they had never pursued conflicting policies; they both proclaimed their hatred of colonialism, and it seemed that they would both be satisfied powers with immense internal resources. If Russia proclaimed her need for a friendly 'buffer' between herself and Germany, and for some guarantees that Germany would never be allowed to attack her again, then surely she had an arguable case which deserved some consideration. The dialectic of Marx and the true nature of communism did not seem to present any insuperable problems to Roosevelt, whose determination to maintain 'Great Power unity' in war and peace continued until his death on April 12th, 1945. On that very day, an hour before he collapsed, he had written of the Berne negotiations (*see note A.3 above*), 'It is my desire to consider the Berne misunderstanding a minor incident.'

How galling it must have been for Churchill throughout the summer to have seen the great rejoicing of the British people, knowing full well that a new crisis was building up in Europe.

2 *The end of the Grand Alliance (ii)*

A *The political atmosphere deteriorated during the immediate post-war months, though this was not fully evident at the Potsdam Conference in July 1945, because:*

(i) Truman and Attlee were both new to the highest office.
(ii) The war in the Far East had not yet been won.

The deterioration, however, became obvious at the Foreign Ministers' Conferences in September and December, 1945, and in the Security Council of the United Nations, which met in January 1946.

B *Great Britain, which bore the brunt of Russian hostility in 1945 and 1946, feared not only Russian penetration into central Europe, but also Russian ambitions in the Middle East and Africa:*

1 March–April 1945. Russia denounced the existing Russo-Turkish treaty of friendship, and later the British Foreign Secretary, Ernest Bevin, resisted Russian demands for the revision of the Montreux Convention of 1936, which, in practice, had allowed real control of the Straits (the Dardanelles and Bosporus) to pass into the hands of Turkey.

2 July 1945. Russia requested trusteeship over one or more of the ex-Italian colonies in Africa.

3 By August 1945, Russian-sponsored governments had been set up in Rumania, Bulgaria and Hungary.

4 Throughout 1945 the Russian evacuation of their forces from northern Iran (Azerbaijan) was delayed, and this operation was not completed until May 1946, despite the fact that all American troops had left Iran in 1945.

5 In the Security Council, Russia denounced the presence of

British troops in Greece, and supported the Syrian and Lebanese demands that British and French troops should evacuate Syria and the Lebanon.

6 May and October 1946. Ships of the British Navy were mined in the Corfu Channel, off the coast of communist Albania.

At that time Greece, Turkey and the Middle East were considered by Great Britain to be within her sphere of influence.

C *Slowly, the U.S.A. realised that she must not withdraw from Europe, and the policy of 'containment' was initiated, restraining Russian expansionism by the establishment of regional pacts:*

1 *Germany*. The British government pointed out that the division of Germany into four occupied zones, together with Russia's policy of dismantling German industry to pay for reparations, was hindering Germany's economic recovery and was thus a burden to the Allies. The U.S.A. therefore agreed to the economic union of the British and American zones from January 1st, 1947. This was regarded by Russia as a violation of the Yalta Agreements.

2 *The Truman Doctrine*. In February 1947, the British government informed the U.S.A. that it could no longer afford its commitments in Greece. These included the maintenance of troops in that country and the granting of financial aid to the unsteady democratic régime.

The U.S.A's reply on March 12th, 1947, has become known as the Truman Doctrine, by which the U.S.A. agreed to support 'the free peoples of the world' against totalitarianism. As part of that policy, the U.S.A. took over the British commitments in Greece and gave military and financial assistance to Turkey.

3 *Marshall Aid*. In a speech at Harvard University on June 5th,

1947, General George Marshall, then American Secretary of State, offered American aid for European economic recovery. This was quickly accepted by western European nations (following the lead given by Ernest Bevin), but Russia condemned it as part of the consolidation of western Europe against itself and its neighbours. That 'Marshall Aid' did more than anything else to save Europe from communism cannot be doubted. It was from this time onward (summer, 1947) that the U.S.A. assumed the leadership of the West in the 'cold war'.

During the years covered by these events, two Englishmen from entirely different social backgrounds and belonging to opposing political parties, set the western world upon the path it has followed ever since.

On August 20th, 1945, in his first speech on foreign policy in the House of Commons, Ernest Bevin stated that 'the basis of the (Labour) government's policy was in keeping with that worked out by the coalition government'. This displeased a number of Labour MP's, who had expected that Bevin would follow a policy more sympathetic to Russia's interpretation of affairs, as had indeed been laid down by the National Executive of the Labour Party at the end of 1944. They were dismayed to learn of the long and bitter verbal duels which took place in the Security Council between Bevin and Molotov, and they challenged the Labour government in the House of Commons to justify its retention of British troops in Greece and in the Middle East. (*See C.2 above.*)

Against these attacks, Bevin stood firm, and by early 1947 he had come to accept Churchill's advocacy of regional pacts to assist in preserving peace. Thus, in those early post-war years, a Labour Foreign Secretary, Ernest Bevin, proved that a Labour government in Great Britain was not incompatible with the maintenance of British interests abroad, and that a socialist Britain would ally with a capitalist U.S.A. against aggressive communism.

Meanwhile, Churchill had broken his self-imposed silence on the menace of communism. In the autumn of 1945 he sent the following telegram to Stalin:

> There is not much comfort in looking on to a future where you and the countries you dominate, plus the communist parties in many other states, are all drawn up on one side, and those who rally to the English-speaking nations and their associates or dominions are on the other. It is quite obvious that their quarrel would tear the world to pieces and that all of us leading men on either side who had anything to do with that would be shamed before history. Even embarking on a long period of suspicions, of abuse and counter-abuse of opposing policies would be a disaster hampering the developments of world prosperity for the masses, which are obtainable only through our trinity.

When this drew no reply, Churchill made his famous speech at Fulton, Missouri in the spring of 1946. In this speech he warned the West of the dangers which faced it, spoke of his doubts about Russian intentions and suggested a 'fraternal association' between the British Commonwealth and the U.S.A. What he had to say shocked and surprised many people. In some circles he was described once again as a 'war-monger' or 'an old war horse who could not get the scent of battle out of his nostrils'. In the U.S.A. at that time, talk of danger and of war seemed out of place when, day after day, American service-men were returning to their homes, and government policy was based upon wholehearted support for the United Nations.

Only a few weeks after the Fulton speech, however, in May 1946, a serious quarrel broke out between the U.S.A. and Russian governments over the question of German reparation deliveries, and this, coupled with the constant use of the veto by Molotov in the Security Council, led the U.S.A. to accept the British view that the leading powers of the West must move closer together if peace were to be preserved.

3 *The policy of containment: its early stages*

A *In 1947, 'containment' applied only to Europe:*

1 The European Recovery Programme, or 'Marshall Aid'. Financial and military assistance was freely given by the United States to prevent further communist encroachment from the east. This was particularly important because:

a Czechoslovakia showed signs of falling under communist rule, which she did after a *coup d'état* in February 1948.

b There were large communist parties in both France and Italy, where unemployment and an unsound currency were leading to discontent.

2 The establishment of United States' bases in Greece, Portugal, Turkey and Spain.

3 The withdrawal of United States' troops from Germany ceased.

B *Elsewhere, in the Middle East, Asia, Africa and South America, there seemed to the Americans no immediate danger of conflict with Russia. Loyal to the Wilsonian doctrine of self-determination for small nations, they led their sometimes reluctant allies in a policy of disengagement:*

1 In the Middle East:

a France reluctantly withdrew from the Lebanon and Syria.

b Great Britain remained in Palestine and Jordan, but withdrew from Iraq (except from some airfields) and from the delta area of Egypt to the Suez Canal Zone. Ernest Bevin even talked of removing the British Army base from the Middle East to Mombasa in Kenya.

c The U.S.A. and Russia withdrew from Iran, though Russia left a subservient government in the north. In September 1947, a United States military mission was established in Teheran.

2 In the Far East:

a Great Britain withdrew from the Indian sub-continent—from India and Pakistan, Burma and Ceylon—and recalled her troops from Indonesia.

b The U.S.A. surrendered her sovereignty over the Philippines and recalled her troops from China.

c Only the Netherlands (in Indonesia), France (in Indo-China), and Portugal (in Goa) refused to give way before the rising tide of nationalism.

3 In Africa, the peoples were considered to be still largely tribal, and not yet politically mature enough to emerge from colonialism or to be tempted by communism.

4 In South America the U.S.A. had exercised undisputed influence since the early nineteenth century.

These newly developing nations would be assisted by:

(i) The British Colombo Plan and President Truman's 'Point Four'—both plans for economic aid.

(ii) The Technical Aid Programme of the United Nations, and other United Nations agencies, such as the World Health Organisation.

C *The Russian point of view was that:*

1 Russia had, for centuries, been attempting to obtain a southern outlet to the sea in the west and a secure frontier, both of which geography had denied her. The setting-up of communist governments in the eastern European states was therefore a defensive measure, protecting Russia against a resurgent Germany. 'Containment' aimed at denying Russia this security and was therefore a policy directed against her reasonable needs. 'Marshall Aid' was a means of resuscitating Germany (a charge sharply refuted by Ernest Bevin in August 1947).

2 Outside Europe, the western Allies were merely substituting 'economic imperialism' for 'political imperialism':

a United States and British economic aid to small nations would bind them firmly into the western trading system.

b Offers of economic aid would be accompanied by demands for military, naval or air bases—e.g. in Greece and Turkey.

3 The United Nations Organisation was becoming a tool of the U.S.A. She had a majority in the General Assembly, and only the Russian veto prevented more of her friends from being elected.

In Great Britain there was some sympathy for this Russian interpretation, but the Labour government as a whole did not accept it and remained a loyal partner of the U.S.A.

4 The policy of containment: the Iron Curtain falls across Europe

A *From late 1947 to 1949 there occurred events which confirmed the division of Europe into opposing camps:*

1 In the East:

a In October 1947, in answer to the Marshall Plan (*see page* 6), Russia created the Cominform, giving some central direction to the communist parties not only in eastern Europe but in France and Italy also.

b In December 1947, a communist government was set up in the mountains of northern Greece. This was given every assistance by Greece's northern neighbours—Albania, Bulgaria and Yugoslavia.

c In February 1948, a Russo-Finnish treaty was signed. Finland was thus forced, to some extent, to bow to the wishes of her powerful neighbour.

d In the same month a communist government was established in Czechoslovakia, an event publicly denounced by the U.S.A., Great Britain and France.

e In June 1948, eight Foreign Ministers from communist countries met in Warsaw to discuss their future policy towards Germany.

f In the same month began the Berlin blockade—cutting off Berlin from western Europe in an effort to force the western Allies to withdraw their forces from the city and to surrender their rights as agreed at Potsdam.

g In August 1948, at a Congress held at Wroclaw (Breslau), the communists set up the Partisans of Peace Organisation. Its object was to prevent western unity by playing up the natural desire for peace which existed in the minds of all citizens.

2 In the West:

a In February 1948, the British, French and U.S. governments began separate talks on the future of Western Germany.

b In March 1948, Great Britain, France, Belgium, the Netherlands and Luxembourg signed the Brussels Treaty. This was a defensive alliance, nominally directed against Germany but adaptable for use against communist aggression.

c In April 1948, at Frankfurt, a constitution for West Germany was put forward.

d In June 1948, the United States Congress voted to give military assistance to allied defence pacts. This would strengthen the Brussels Treaty.

e In June 1948 also, the western governments determined to break the Berlin blockade and began a massive 'airlift' to carry supplies to west Berlin.

B *Meanwhile, the Foreign Ministers' Conferences had been abandoned:*

Not one was held between November 1947 and May 1949, so that all hopes of an Austrian peace treaty faded, and Austria remained occupied by the four powers. In the United Nations, communists and western delegates abused each other with growing bitterness.

C *In June 1948, after many hostile exchanges between Stalin and Tito, Yugoslavia was expelled from the Cominform, with the following results:*

1 Stalin now had a new potential enemy.

2 The western Allies saw that the communist bloc was not so united as it appeared on the surface.

3 President Tito closed the Yugoslav frontier with Greece, and the Greek communist government in the north collapsed. The Greek civil war was thus at an end.

4 The U.S.A. now offered aid to Yugoslavia, which was accepted.

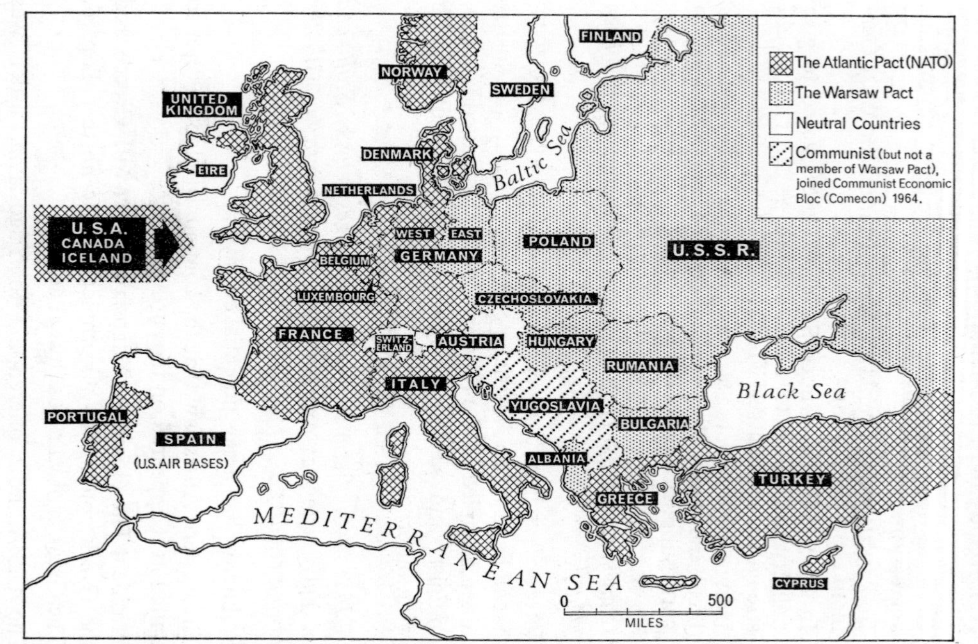

1 The Atlantic Pact (NATO) and the Warsaw Pact

D *The 'Iron Curtain' had now fallen across Europe:*

In the West:

On April 4th, 1949, the North Atlantic Treaty Organisation came into being. The treaty was signed by the U.S.A., Canada and ten western European powers, who stressed that its purpose was solely to preserve the peace by resisting aggression.

In the East:

The Russian government was not overawed by the creation of NATO, and, had it wished to do so, could probably have advanced into western Europe later in 1949, especially when it became known that Russia now possessed the atomic bomb. In fact, Russia directed her efforts:

a Against Yugoslavia.

b Towards the consolidation of the Peoples' Democracies. For example:

(i) There were purges in Hungary, Bulgaria, Albania, Poland and Czechoslovakia.

(ii) The leaders of the Roman Catholic Church in eastern European countries were attacked. (Cardinal Mindszenty in Hungary.)

It was the uncertainty of her satellites rather than the strength of NATO which, if anything, deterred Russia in 1949–50.

E *The real achievement of NATO was to give renewed confidence to the peoples of western Europe, with the following results:*

1 The feeling that war was inevitable gradually faded.

2 The British, United States and French governments were more determined than ever to succeed in setting up a democratic régime in West Germany.

3 The end of the Berlin blockade in May 1949 seemed to be a triumph for the policy of consolidation and concerted action by the West.

4 The West now renewed negotiations with Russia, and a new Foreign Ministers' Conference was held in May and June 1949. Nothing conclusive was decided and there were no further meetings until March 1951.

There can be no doubt that the North Atlantic Treaty gave stability and direction to post-war British foreign policy. Until then, despite the acrimonious arguments which took place with unfailing regularity in the Security Council, the British had been forced, in the absence of any powerful alternative, to look to the United Nations as the only organisation which might preserve the peace. It is true that, from the beginning, many people in Great Britain felt sceptical about the ability of the United Nations in this direction. The news of its inception at San Francisco in 1945 was received coolly in Great Britain, to say the least, and many observers quickly began to realize that its constitution was not drawn up to meet the contingencies of the 'cold war'—but what was to replace it?

From 1947 to 1949, British and western foreign policy was untidy. The countries of the West were travelling vaguely in the same direction; the western European nations strengthened themselves within their own limited means by the Brussels Treaty, the Council of Europe and the organisation for European Economic Co-operation. The U.S.A. had given Europe hope as a result of the Marshall Plan, and had assumed responsibilities in Europe which would have been considered out of the question in 1945; but, as yet, there was no Atlantic Community.

The North Atlantic Treaty Organisation knit Europe and the U.S.A. together, and at the same time, its defensive character quietened uneasy consciences. It could never become an 'instrument of liberation', but it could and did develop into the 'main guardian of the purposes and principles of the Charter'. In providing a balance to the great Russian armies of the east, it would preserve the peace, and, additionally, it might create the atmosphere in which the United Nations could become 'a more effective centre for harmonising the actions of nations'.

2 Pre-war and post-war Germany

5 The policy of containment: the German problem

A *In Germany, the boundary between the western zones of occupation and the Russian zone had become part of the dividing line between communist and non-communist Europe (the Iron Curtain):*

1 In the West:

a In June 1948, the western powers introduced a reform of the currency in their zones of occupation, and the West German Director of Economics, Herr Erhard, lifted some controls from internal trade. This quickly improved conditions in the western zones of Germany and gave new heart to the German people.

b An occupation statute had been promulgated which united the American, British and French zones from April 1949.

c In May 1949, the state parliaments of the Länder accepted a basic law, establishing the German Federal Republic and arranging for the first federal elections. This German Federal Republic would have its capital in Bonn.

d In August 1949, as a result of the elections, Dr Adenauer and his Christian Democratic Union were elected to form a government, having narrowly defeated Dr Schumacher and the Social Democrats.

e In September 1950, the western Allies proclaimed the end of the state of war with Germany.

2 In the East:

a In May 1949, the German Democratic Republic was established, after its constitution had been accepted by the East German people through a referendum.

b In October 1949, Herr Grotewohl became the communist leader of this 'People's Republic'.

B *These moves heightened the tension between East and West:*

1 Neither side would recognise the legitimacy of what the other

had done, the West maintaining that only the refusal of the Russians to allow free elections in East Germany prevented unification.

2 Because the fear of Russia was now greater in the West than the fear of a resurgent Germany, the first steps were soon to be taken to admit German forces to the western defence system:

a In November 1949, West Germany was admitted to the Council of Europe.

b In May 1950, West Germany became a member of the European Coal and Steel Community (Schuman Plan).

c In October 1950, the Allies attempted to create a European Defence Community (Plevin Plan), which would include German forces. This failed when France refused to ratify the plan in August 1954, but the West did not have to wait long before the idea of rearming West Germany was accepted. In October 1954, West Germany was admitted to NATO, and the Western European Union was created.

3 The West was growing increasingly confident that German militarism could be controlled by the setting up of supra-national European institutions, and the first steps towards a united Europe were therefore taken, but:

a On the other side of the Iron Curtain, Russia and her allies, especially Poland and Czechoslovakia, now feared a renewal of German aggression more than ever.

b There was the danger that West Germany might attempt the reunification of all Germany by force.

c There was also the danger that West Germany might lead her allies in an attempt to regain the territories east of the Oder–Neisse line and in the Sudetenland.

To prevent these dangers, the eastern powers thought it necessary to establish communism in East Germany quickly, and to eliminate what they considered to be the potential allies of the West Germans in the east, i.e. the large land-owners and industrialists.

C *Berlin, which lay in the centre of the Russian zone of Germany, had been divided into four sectors and was administered by the great powers. It could be reached from the west only by air, by canal, railway or autobahn:*

1 On June 24th, 1948, the Russians closed the overland routes from West Germany to Berlin for the following reasons:

a They disliked having an island of western civilisation on the eastern side of the Iron Curtain, which was then falling into place across Europe.

b They hoped that by driving the U.S.A., Great Britain and France from Berlin, they would destroy the confidence which was growing between the West Germans and their newly won allies. This in turn would put an end to the economic recovery of West Germany and to the plans for a West German government.

2 The Berlin blockade lasted for eleven months, during which time an Anglo-American airlift saved the western sectors of the city from starvation ('Operation Vittles' as the Americans called it). A western counter-blockade caused a shortage of raw materials in East Germany.

3 Despite attempts at mediation through the United Nations, it was not until May 11th, 1949 that a settlement was found. By that time, however, the West Germans were convinced that it would be in their best interests to postpone the unification of Germany in favour of setting up a West German state in alliance with the western powers.

It is interesting to note that the first sign that Russia might be willing to reconsider her terms for raising the Berlin blockade came from an American journalist who was granted an interview by Stalin on January 27th, 1949. Previously, the main stumbling block in all negotiations had been the question of the type of currency to be used in west Berlin. At this interview, Stalin discussed Berlin and his terms for ending the blockade, but he did not mention the currency question, and soon the corridors of the United Nations building were buzzing with speculation. The deputy American representative on the Security Council approached Mr Malik as he was sitting in the delegates' lounge, cables were sent to Moscow and from the replies it was soon obvious that successful negotiations might be launched.

It is not likely that Russia's change of heart had been brought about by anything the United Nations had done, but the Berlin blockade had helped to clarify the true position of the United Nations as it stood in 1949. It had become obvious that no pressure from neutrals, nor any intervention by the Secretary-General, would have any effect unless the great powers wished to compromise. On the other hand, when normal diplomatic channels were closed by the bitter feelings between the powers, the United Nations provided a permanent point of contact between East and West which could be used as soon as the time was ripe. Without this point of contact, and without the steady moral pressure which the United Nations exerted, the Berlin question could have plunged the world into war in 1949. (*For further notes on Berlin, see Chapter 10, page 48.*)

6 *Great Britain's need of alliances in post-war Europe*

A *British governments have always disliked the idea of continuing alliances in peacetime:*

1 In 1815 Castlereagh tried to bring about a closer association with Europe through the Congress system, but this proved a failure as far as Great Britain was concerned.

2 Throughout the nineteenth century, Great Britain engaged in no permanent alliances, and towards the end of the century she followed a policy of 'splendid isolation'.

3 With the Boer War and the build-up of the two 'armed camps' in Europe (The Dual Alliance of France and Russia and the Triple Alliance of Germany, Austria and Italy), it became necessary for Great Britain to secure her interests by formal treaties. Even then, however, the British government entered into friendly *ententes* rather than defensive alliances (e.g. The *Entente Cordiale* with France in 1904).

4 Between the two world wars formal alliances were again abandoned, and British statesmen put their faith in the doctrine of 'collective security' as promised in the covenant of the League of Nations. When this failed to deal with Japanese, Italian and German aggression, Great Britain had to enter into a new series of alliances which culminated in the victory of 1945.

5 In the immediate post-war world it was hoped that the United Nations Organisation would succeed where the League of Nations had failed, though it was realised from the start that everything would depend upon the willingness of the great powers to work together. Great Britain and the U.S.A. (which also had a tradition of isolationism) had to enter, once again, into permanent defensive alliances:

a *Treaty of Dunkirk:* Great Britain and France—March 1947.

b *Treaty of Brussels:* Great Britain, France, Belgium, Luxembourg and the Netherlands—March 1948.

c *The North Atlantic Treaty*: Great Britain, the U.S.A., Canada and nine European countries—April 1949.

d *The European Defence Community:* France, Germany, Belgium, the Netherlands, Luxembourg and Italy—May 1952.

Though Great Britain 'explained her inability to become a member of the Community' because of her overseas interests, she did promise close support, and so did the U.S.A. The treaty failed however, when the French Assembly, not yet prepared to risk German rearmament nor yet to surrender any sovereignty to a supra-national authority, refused to ratify it in August 1954.

e *Western European Union:* Great Britain, France, Belgium, the Netherlands, Luxembourg, Italy and West Germany—October 1954.

This replaced the European Defence Community. It provided that Great Britain would guarantee to maintain four divisions and a strategic air command in Europe, and it allowed for limited German rearmament with conventional weapons only. No surrender of national sovereignty was involved. In Great Britain, the Labour party abstained from voting on this agreement, because it was known that at least seventy-two Labour MP's would refuse to agree to German rearmament. In September 1954, the official leadership of the Labour party had only narrowly defeated a motion against German rearmament at the annual conference.

B *Difficulties continue to exist between Great Britain and her European allies for various reasons:*

1 European states have always objected to the special importance which Great Britain attaches to her alliance with the U.S.A. and to her possession of her own nuclear deter-

rent. France, especially, demands parity with Great Britain, and this has led to her own development of nuclear weapons, to her *force de frappe*, and to her demands for reform of the NATO organisation. (*See pages 29 and 47.*)

2 During the years when Europe was moving towards political and economic unity, Great Britain was accused of 'dragging her feet'. The creation of the European Free Trade Area was considered by some to be a British attempt to return to her traditional policy of balancing power in Europe by keeping it divided. (*See page 192.*)

3 Great Britain has been accused of failing to live up to her European commitments because she is fundamentally a world power, with many overseas and Commonwealth interests.

7 The problems facing the North Atlantic Treaty Organisation

NATO was conceived as a regional pact, under Article 51 of the United Nations Charter, for the defence of member nations against Russian aggression. In the second half of the twentieth century, however, this was impossible unless national interests were subordinated to the well-being of the organisation. So far, this had not wholly been the case:

A *The intervention by Great Britain and France at Suez in 1956 (see pages 142–8) was carried out in the face of opposition from the U.S.A. and without reference to the wishes of other NATO members:*

It is significant that this episode occurred after the unanimous appointment of a committee of 'Three Wise Men' (Martino, Lange and Pearson) to consider how to bring about 'greater unity in NATO in the non-military field'. Though the dangers of the Suez entanglement led to the acceptance of far-reaching proposals by this committee, they were, in fact, not successful in strengthening the Organisation.

B *In 1955 the British Defence White Paper announced the production of the thermo-nuclear bomb, and though the need for Great Britain's alliances (NATO, WEU, etc.) was said to be as great as ever, a new series of difficulties within NATO was about to arise:*

1 Great Britain had always been anxious to confirm the 'special relationship' which she had with the U.S.A. The fact that Great Britain and the U.S.A. would now both be 'nuclear powers' gave added point to this position and caused jealousy amongst the other NATO powers, also the

determination, in France at least, to develop nuclear weapons of her own.

2 In the late 1950's, Mr Sandys, the British Defence Minister, without consulting his allies in NATO, developed a defence policy which altered the balance of power within the alliance. He argued that in future, the NATO powers should contribute to collective defence in the manner best suited to their own arms positions. Since Great Britain and the U.S.A. already had nuclear weapons, they should be relied upon to provide the nuclear deterrent, implying, at the same time, that the other nations in the alliance should provide the conventional ground forces. To this end, Mr Sandys stepped up the production of the British nuclear deterrent, but at the same time he abandoned conscription and proposed reductions in the size of the British Army of the Rhine. This policy was disliked at SHAPE and it caused some Europeans to claim that once more, 'Great Britain intended to fight to the last Frenchman'.

Further White papers from 1958 to 1962, however, in the main continued to support Mr Sandys' argument, despite the decision to stop production of the 'Blue Streak' missile and to purchase American 'Skybolt' and later 'Polaris' missiles. It was said that 'the concept of interdependence' required NATO to 'get away from the idea that each member nation must continue to maintain self-contained national forces which, by themselves, are fully balanced'. Critics of Great Britain, however, claim that this respectable philosophy of collective defence seems to conceal a determination on the part of Great Britain to retain her 'great power' status relative to the other fourteen NATO powers.

3 The Anglo-American agreement in Nassau in December 1962, by which Great Britain was to be supplied with American 'Polaris' missiles ('Skybolt' having proved a

failure), and the break-up of the Common Market talks in Brussels during January 1963, brought to an end all hopes of a European deterrent which might have gone into action if and when the American nuclear shield was withdrawn from its transatlantic role, and which might have dissolved the mistrust felt in Europe for Great Britain.

This forced NATO to look once again to the fundamental problem facing alliances in the nuclear age. If individual states refuse to surrender their sovereignty, what form of control of nuclear weapons will provide the maximum protection to all? At the Ottawa Conference in May 1963, the NATO Ministers considered two alternative suggestions which might overcome this difficulty.

The first proposed the establishment of a multi-national force to which individual countries would contribute, with the right of recall in the event of a supreme national emergency. The British government quickly agreed to put its V-bomber force at the disposal of this new organisation, but, together with other allies, it has yet to accept the idea of a multi-lateral force which would so mix national contributions that individual recall would be impossible. This was the second proposal tabled for discussion at Ottawa, and in spite of early scepticism, the first such force to come into existence could be a nuclear surface fleet with ships manned by crews of more than one nation. If such a nuclear force were made to work, it might well prove to be a new stimulus to interdependence which, as we have said, has so far been accepted more in theory than in practice. But during 1964–65 East-West relations and the political position in Western Europe underwent such a change that neither a M.L.F. nor an A.N.F. were of such immediate significance. Both might be replaced by the creation of a NATO Nuclear Committee, which would have the advantage of unifying the Alliance whilst preserving the possibility of an agreement with Russia to stop the spread of nuclear weapons—something not conceivable so long as the Soviet leaders fear the acquisition or control of atomic weapons by West Germany.

C *In 1958 President de Gaulle rejected the idea of military integration in NATO, withdrew the French Mediterranean Fleet and most of the French Air Force from NATO command and accelerated the development of French nuclear bombs:*

It was suggested that this nationalistic policy was necessary if de Gaulle were to bring about peace in Algeria, where the war against the Algerian nationalists had been the cause of embarrassment to the alliance as a whole, as well as a source of strength to communist propagandists in the West. It is also probable, however, that the refusal of the U.S.A. to share with her allies the control of nuclear warheads was a blow to their pride and provoked a nationalistic response which militated against the unity of NATO.

D *Developments in Africa were also the cause of much mistrust between the fifteen NATO powers:*

In that continent 'the wind of change' brought new nations into existence, and because some members were—and some still are—imperial powers, the rate at which they were willing to give way before the rise of African nationalism was not always uniform. At the same time, the traditional anti-colonialism of the U.S.A. led their government to endeavour to outbid the communists by backing African nationalist leaders against the European nations. This caused bitter feelings within the alliance over such matters as the Congo crisis, where it was felt that Belgium should have taken her allies into her confidence before abdicating her position in that region, and where the support of the U.S.A. for the United Nations in Katanga was, at times, in direct opposition to the policies of the British and other European governments. (*See pages 162–8.*)

Another example of internal NATO conflict was to be found in Angola, where the actions of the Portuguese government in putting down a native uprising were condemned by Adlai Stevenson, who voted against Portugal in the United Nations.

E *Lastly, there were many other examples of the strength of nationalism within the Atlantic Alliance:*

Greeks and Turks almost came to blows over Cyprus, Great Britain and Iceland became involved in a fisheries dispute, and the creation of the European Free Trade Area, at Great Britain's instigation, seemed to confirm some European states in their suspicions that 'perfidious Albion' did not wish to see a united Europe, let alone become a part of it.

It is true that some of these problems settled themselves. Peace was made in Algeria and the allies came to accept the policy of the United Nations in the Congo and in Cyprus, but in the mid-1960's France still exploded her atomic bombs and Great Britain continued to rely upon her independent deterrent. The doctrine of interdependence, however, gradually became more of a reality.

F *There is also the German problem, which has been the cause of embarrassment for many years:*

It was and still is impossible to forget and forgive the crimes of Nazism. Some NATO countries have succeeded in doing this more than others. President de Gaulle was determined to put an end to Franco-German hostility, and met with great success, which is the more commendable when one remembers the refusal of the French National Assembly to ratify the treaty which would have set up a European Defence Community in 1954, and the continued efforts of M. Mendès-France to keep West Germany out of NATO. In fact, of course, the arguments in favour of West Germany's participation were overwhelming. NATO needed more manpower if Russia's numerical supremacy were to be countered effectively, and from a strategic point of view, the allied armies needed more room to manœuvre if they were to withstand and defeat an enemy offensive.

The vital question, however, was always how to bring German re-armament under effective European control. Had the European Defence Community been acceptable to the French National Assembly, West Germany would have retained much less sovereignty than she has today. Indeed, since the German Federal Republic joined NATO on October 22nd, 1954, and became a member of the Western European Union which was set up on the next day, she has exercised a greater influence in the councils of Europe than was ever expected.

West Germany, indeed, has often been regarded as 'America's best friend in Europe', and most NATO powers have been worried lest her armies should be equipped with atomic weapons. Moreover, the division of Germany and the isolation of west Berlin have been major factors in the 'cold war'. Even in the early 1960's, the NATO governments could not speak with an entirely united voice in promising to defend west Berlin. There were still those who could see no reason to risk a nuclear war for the sake of ex-enemies. Indeed, though any signs of renewed Nazi activities were generally dealt with speedily by the German authorities, many ex-Nazis still held positions of power, and this proved to be not only an effective communist propaganda weapon, but helped to keep alive the mistrust and suspicion of Germany which then existed.

In 1958, President Heuss was received with little enthusiasm by the British people when he made a state visit to London. In 1959, Chancellor Adenauer criticised those sections of the British public who withheld their friendship from the new democratic Germany, and in 1961 at the time of the Berlin crisis, some Labour MP's tabled a motion of censure on the government for allowing West German troops to train in Pembrokeshire.

This anti-German feeling was probably more widespread in Great Britain than anywhere else in the Atlantic Alliance. As far as NATO was concerned, however, it was bound to be a cause of weakness and was a problem which gave some concern.

G *The fifteen members of NATO did not form a natural group:* They had no natural frontiers, Scandinavia was divided in two, Germany was split down the middle, Portugal, Greece and Turkey were isolated geographically from their allies, and neutral Switzerland and Austria caused difficulties of communication. In 1950 it was felt that the original twelve members of NATO could truly be said to constitute an Atlantic Community, with the ocean as the unifying factor; but then Greece, Turkey and the German Federal Republic became members and it was obvious that NATO was primarily a defensive military alliance. It was also obvious that Article 2 of the treaty, which called for political and economic co-operation, was likely to be the most difficult part to put into effect.

The war against communism, however, was not always to be a 'hot' one. Communism advanced because it appealed to the under-privileged, to some who saw in it the answer to the inequalities of life, and to many who were affected by the fundamental optimism of the communist. History was on his side—he could not fail, however long he might take to win! One of the major problems facing NATO in the early 1960's was to discover and to state with sincerity what it was that the alliance stood for. This task was not made easier by the use of platitudes such as 'the defence of freedom' or 'the defence of the free world', because if freedom were a prerogative of western democracies, then Turkey and Portugal should never have been accepted as members of NATO, and the United States House of Representatives should never have voted in favour of the admission of Spain to NATO, as it did in July 1955. Some people believe that the Atlantic Alliance was strong enough by the mid-1960's, militarily speaking, to insist upon the highest moral and ethical standards for its members. The U.S.A. no longer needed bases in territories where the maintenance of right-wing dictatorships seemed the only answer to communist subversion. Towards this end, some thought that the Polaris submarine might have a significant role to play, not only as an ultimate military weapon (if there is such a thing) but as a means of strengthening the West from the moral point of view.

H *On May 11th, 1953, two months after the death of Stalin, Sir Winston Churchill suggested a conference with the Russian government 'at the highest level', and from then on, the NATO allies were divided amongst themselves over the question of whether or not to talk to the Russians at a 'Summit Conference':*

The conferences held at Geneva in 1955 and at Paris in 1960 were such failures that Great Britain, who pursued the idea more faithfully than anyone else, was accused of appeasement by the Germans, French and Americans, and this lack of unity amongst the allies must have been most pleasing to Mr Khrushchev and his associates.

There can be little doubt that any further negotiations between East and West will be preceded by months of preparation carried out in private at ambassadorial level.

I *The question of nuclear disarmament:*

There were many individuals whose countries belonged to NATO who were horrified at the new weapons of mass destruction upon which the alliance depends. Their activities in protest against the use of such weapons, received considerable publicity and their sincerity was often beyond doubt. But they provided a rallying cry for dissent within the alliance and it was possible at one time that their belief in unilateral disarmament might become more widespread in the West, or, alternatively, that their significance might be entirely over-estimated by the Russian government. Either way, they were a problem which caused NATO some concern until the improvement of relations between Russia and the U.S.A. which followed the crisis over Cuba in October 1962 (*pages 176–80*) and the partial Test Ban Treaty of August 5th, 1963.

The establishment of a 'hot line' (i.e. direct telephonic communication between the White House and the Kremlin) tended to remove the immediate threat of nuclear war which had horrified so many people and given point to their protests.

8 The problems of peaceful co-existence

A *Two main factors have combined to produce the policy of 'peaceful co-existence' which Mr Khrushchev initiated in 1956:*

1 The development of atomic weapons had made nonsense of the earlier belief that 'war is merely the continuation of diplomacy by other means'. No one could win a nuclear war, though Communist China refused to subscribe to this view.

2 At the twentieth Soviet Communist Party Congress of 1956, Mr Khrushchev declared that war between Russia and the rest of the non-communist world was not 'fatalistically inevitable', as Marxist-Leninism had previously taught. Mr Khrushchev affirmed that victory for communism was certain, but he proclaimed that 'Socialism does not require war to spread its ideals . . . war cannot and must not serve as a means of settling international disputes'.

B *Though there can be no doubt that 'peaceful co-existence' was preferable to the Stalinist belief that a communist victory could only be secured through war, it is right that everyone should understand the nature of the new Russian policy:*

1 It did not mean that Russia, whose foreign policy could nearly always be identified with the advance of international communism, had agreed to accept a *status quo* situation of 'live and let live'.

2 It meant that Russia would attempt to defeat responsible government and a mixed (or free) economy by all the means in her power short of war—propaganda, exploitation of industrial unrest by the communist party, intense campaigns of slander against the West, economic aid to backward countries with no obvious strings attached—all these methods and many others, some definitely subversive, would be used to bring about the ultimate victory of the communist ideology.

C *The pursuit of this policy by the Russian government led to tension between Russia and China:*

It was generally thought, however, that there existed between those two countries an 'inviolable and eternal alliance' and that it would be unwise to exaggerate the differences which undoubtedly existed. Nonetheless Mao Tse-tung spoke of China as the only country capable of withstanding a nuclear war, and there can be no doubt that the Chinese government saw some aspects of 'peaceful co-existence' (such as any *rapprochement* between East and West, however tactical it might be from the Russian point of view) as the work of 'dangerous deviationists'. The Sino-Russian dispute grew worse after Mr Khrushchev refused to plunge the world into nuclear war and agreed to withdraw Russian missiles from Cuba (*see pages 176–80*).

Russia's fear of China undoubtedly helped to promote the favourable atmosphere for the three-power talks which led to the Partial Test Ban Treaty of August 5th, 1963 (*see page 45*) and its possible consequences. It may be that Russia will be forced to return to more rigid and unyielding policies towards the West in order to appease her Oriental neighbour, but it could be that Mr Khrushchev agreed with President Kennedy when he said that China's strength in the 1970's might create 'a more dangerous situation than any we have faced since the end of the Second World War'. A Russian diplomat is reported to have said that if the Sino-Russian quarrel were basically one of the interpretation of Marxist-Leninism, then it might be possible to heal it over a period of time. If, on the other hand, the Chinese have racialist ambitions, there could be no agreement.

D *On September 23rd, 1960, Mr Khrushchev, addressing the United Nations General Assembly, said that the Russian foreign policy towards the newly emerged states of Asia, Africa and*

Latin America meant 'sincere friendship and great mutual understanding and respect, the rendering of economic and technical assistance to less developed countries, without any attempt to impose upon them political or military commitments'.

This statement, and others like it, have provoked the following reactions from Western statesmen:

1 They state that the Russian conception of truth differed from that accepted in the West. Mr Khrushchev did not openly make political demands upon new nations in exchange for financial or technical assistance, but the infiltration of communism into their political and economic systems would be gradual and almost indiscernible.

For example, cotton provides 80 per cent of Egypt's exports, and between 1956 and 1958 Russia began to buy between 60 per cent and 70 per cent of Egypt's total cotton production at prices well above world market levels. This naturally excluded all other prospective buyers, and it became obvious to President Nasser that unless something were done quickly, his country would soon be entirely dependent upon Russia for its economic livelihood. This accounts for the *rapprochement* between Egypt and the West which began in 1959, and it supports Marshal Tito's theory that an uncommitted nation can only remain truly independent if one-third of its trade is with the West, one-third with the communist bloc, and one-third with the neutrals.

2 Other Western statesmen have pointed out that the West is always at a disadvantage if it attempts to compete with the communists for the goodwill of the new nations, because:

a European governments have been (and some still are) associated with colonialism and exploitation.

b Most new nations wish for speedy industrialisation, which demands planning. They see the successes in Russia and China and they are deeply impressed. Consequently, they are often willing to surrender ideas of political liberty (which they have never experienced in practice) in order that material benefits may be won.

c In the past, western governments have demanded political, military or economic concessions in return for protection against communism. Such demands have led to embarrassments in the Middle East, in Laos, South Korea and elsewhere, and such policy often offended the tender nationalism of the new states. For the time being, however, it was made necessary by the policy of containment which was being pursued.

E *The draft programme of the Communist Party of the Soviet Union, published in July 1961, states that 'The Soviet Union is not pursuing the task of communist construction alone, but in fraternal association with the other Socialist states.'*

Most of these other Socialist states are in eastern Europe, which was 'liberated' by Russian troops in 1945. During Stalin's lifetime the communist ideology was forced upon them and they were exploited economically for the benefit of Russia. Risings in East Germany (1953) and in Hungary (1956) were ruthlessly suppressed, and though conditions improved in the years which followed, peoples in these countries were never allowed to choose freely their own form of government. As far as peaceful co-existence was concerned, the political future of these eastern European states was not negotiable. Communism was established by right of military conquest and Russia would fight rather than tolerate the rebirth of any western ideals in these areas.

F *The problem of Berlin has been a potential danger since the airlift broke the blockade in 1949, but it became a more immediate threat to peace when Mr Khrushchev announced that it must be settled to his satisfaction by the end of 1961 (for further details see Chapter 10, page 48).*

Here it must be noted that the questions of Berlin, disengagement in central Europe and disarmament were probably the most vital issues to be settled if 'peaceful co-existence', even as the communists understand it, were not to degenerate into nuclear war.

9 Disarmament and disengagement

A *Since its inception in 1945, the United Nations Organisation held, and has continued to hold, a series of conferences on the subject of disarmament:*

At first, the United Nations was charged only with the task of 'regulating' armaments, but since 1954, when it was known that both the U.S.A. and Russia had successfully exploded hydrogen bombs, the subject took on a new intensity, for world opinion demanded that statesmen at least pay lip-service to the idea of bringing the arms race to an end.

Despite the horror of nuclear warfare, however, and the fears of the effects of 'fall-out' (radiation), there remained a degree of scepticism in the minds of even the most optimistic observers:

1 Those who remembered the 1930's knew that Fascist dictators drew strength from the military weaknesses of the rest of Europe.

2 There was also a feeling that the arms race was not a cause, but a consequence, of international tension. If this view were accepted, it would be obvious that there could be no real disarmament until the German problem was solved and policies for co-existence had been proved workable.

3 The representatives at disarmament conferences faced terrible problems, but because they had to negotiate in the glare of world opinion, their task was made more difficult. Mr Anthony Nutting recorded that in his view, real agreement had never been a practical possibility, for each side sought popular support by putting forward suggestions which the other side was unlikely to accept. On the rare occasions when proposals were made which might prove acceptable, they were always hastily withdrawn.

4 It was pointed out that the world was living under the *pax*

atomica—the 'great deterrent'. People continue to worry about 'whose finger is on the trigger' but the threat of 'massive and instant retaliation' (Dulles) had already preserved the peace of the world for years and 'might lead, not to general annihilation, but to the outlawry of war, which generation after generation has hitherto sought in vain'.

5 Disarmament would mean a major economic revolution in the west, for financial stability depends to some extent upon obtaining defence orders. Only the greatest cynics put this forward as a major reason for the failure of statesmen to find a solution to the problem of disarmament. But it is true that, if and when disarmament is accepted, it may have to be phased and timed so that governments can make the necessary plans to deal with a difficult period in their national economies.

B *Little value would be achieved by examining in detail the disarmament negotiations which went on since 1945. Briefly, they fell into easily distinguishable periods:*

1 *1945–1949* When the United Nations Disarmament Commission examined the Baruch Plan for an International Atomic Agency, and other plans submitted by Russia, which aimed at the destruction of all atomic weapons and a reduction in conventional forces.

2 *1950–1953* At this time, because of the Korean war, a general wave of rearmament was sweeping over the world. Strangely enough, this was the period when Russia agreed to the principle of international inspection, provided that all nuclear and conventional weapons were included in the overall disarmament plan.

3 *1954–1955* The successful explosion of hydrogen bombs by the U.S.A. and Russia led to a meeting on May 13th, 1954, of the Disarmament Sub-Committee at Lancaster House in

London to consider an Anglo-French plan. Though both Mr Vishinsky and Mr Malik showed some signs of wanting an agreement, it soon became obvious that the conference would fail, because no effective means of control over manufacture was acceptable.

The question was taken up again, however, at the Geneva Summit Meeting on July 21st, 1955, when Eisenhower, Bulganin, Eden and Faure submitted plans for consideration. In the event, none of these proved acceptable, but a distinct change of emphasis had appeared in the negotiations. From now on, the Commission would pay a greater attention to the idea of partial disarmament as opposed to a comprehensive plan, whilst, at the highest level, attempts would be made (perhaps by further Summit Meetings) to increase confidence between powers by the removal of political difficulties.

4 *1956–1958* During this period, plans for the suspension of nuclear tests were put forward at the same time as ideas for 'disengagement in central Europe'. In December 1956, Hugh Gaitskell, the leader of the British Labour Party, suggested the idea of 'a large neutral area which would be guaranteed by a security pact and from which armed forces would be withdrawn, both on the Russian side and on our side'. He was joined in October 1957, by Adam Rapacki, the Polish Foreign Minister, who suggested setting up an 'atom-free' zone in central Europe, covering many miles on both sides of the 'Iron Curtain'.

Neither of these plans was acceptable to the governments of the great powers, but some work was done at Geneva in exchanging views on the subject of suspension of nuclear tests. Some months later, however, the conference adjourned after having failed to agree on the question of international inspection—considered by Russia to be a device to conceal espionage by the West.

5 *1958–1962* On May 18th, 1960, Mr Khrushchev destroyed all hope of a successful Summit Meeting. The reasons for this are to be found elsewhere (*pages* 202–4), but as might be expected, his action foreshadowed a bleak and dangerous period in East-West relations. Nevertheless, the election of John F. Kennedy to the Presidency of the U.S.A. marked a slight improvement, and a voluntary moratorium on nuclear tests, accepted by all nuclear powers except France, seemed to augur well for the future. Following the Berlin crisis of August 1961, however, the Russians announced a return to testing, and during the following weeks, exploded bombs of immense power. In spite of Anglo-American indignation and a cool reception from the neutrals, Mr Khrushchev persisted with this change of policy. He might have been forced into it by the demands of his military advisers, who always insisted that Russia must go on testing until a nuclear balance had been achieved.

In 1961–62, it was certain that, for all her success in space, Russia still lagged far behind the U.S.A. in nuclear striking power. (It might have been to rectify this at one stroke that Khrushchev put missiles into Cuba. *See pages* 176–80.) For equally understandable reasons, the resumption of American nuclear tests was inevitable from September 1961 onwards. It had been her belief since the end of the Second World War that her security depended upon maintaining a complete superiority in the nuclear field over any potential aggressor. A balance of power would not suffice. Indeed, should such a situation develop, the U.S.A. would consider herself to be under the threat of immediate attack. Thus the U.S.A. also resumed nuclear tests, and negotiations at Geneva stumbled slowly forward with little or no chance of success.

6 *From the Cuban crisis of 1962* The situation was fundamentally changed, however, by the Cuban crisis of 1962 (*see*

page 176) and the new developments which followed it. On the afternoon of Wednesday, October 25th, 1962, the world was on the brink of nuclear war, and the recognition of this fact in Washington and Moscow led President Kennedy and Mr Khrushchev to make a reappraisal of the nuclear balance which then existed, and to open a long and secret correspondence about how to end the 'cold war' and remove the dangers of nuclear destruction. They were aided by several significant factors which had entered world politics:

a Defence experts in Russia and the U.S.A. had begun to consider the necessity of embarking upon new and expensive weapons systems of doubtful military value (e.g. the anti-missile missile) at a time when there was a growing demand throughout the world for an improved standard of living. Increased expenditure upon nuclear armaments would be difficult to justify, not only to the leaders of the under-developed countries, who were then becoming more influential in the United Nations Organisation, but also to the people of Russia who had come to expect more consumer goods in the shops.

b The quarrel between China and Russia intensified after the Cuban crisis, despite Mr Khrushchev's attempts to find a practical solution to it. It culminated in a letter of June 14th, 1963, from the Chinese Central Committee to the Soviet Central Committee, which made any settlement seem out of the question. This, as much as anything, accelerated the movement away from the 'cold war'.

Meanwhile, in the West, President de Gaulle rejected the leadership of the U.S.A. when, despite pressure from President Kennedy, he refused Great Britain entry into the E.E.C. (*see page* 198) and when he continued to develop independent French nuclear weapons.

Thus the 'two-bloc' world of the post-war years was breaking up, and a new and terrible danger appeared—the extension of nuclear weapons to countries refusing the leadership of Russia or the U.S.A. This made it more imperative than ever to find some way of bringing the arms race to a halt, for, as President Kennedy said, 1963 might provide the 'last chance' to get a nuclear Test Ban Treaty and an international agreement to check the spread of nuclear weapons.

It was, then, against this more hopeful background that steps were finally taken at Geneva to establish the 'hot line' (direct communication) between the White House and the Kremlin; and arrangements were made for talks in Moscow between Russia, the U.S.A. and Great Britain to negotiate a Partial Test Ban Treaty and to explore other means of reducing tension.

The result of these meetings was the Partial Test Ban Treaty of August 5th, 1963, which forbade all nuclear tests on land, sea or in the air, but allowed the continuation of underground tests, because no agreement could be reached about international inspection. It also contained an escape clause which might be called into play if East–West relations deteriorated once again. This provided that 'if extraordinary events, related to the subject matter of this treaty, have jeopardised the supreme interests of its country', a party to the agreement might resume testing.

The treaty was signed by many powers, including West Germany, but both France and China refused to consider it. This, and the fact that it was not immediately followed up by a non-aggression pact, by measures against surprise attack, by provision against the spread of nuclear weapons or by an agreed limitation of defence budgets, curbed the jubilation which was felt at the time and led to a more cautious estimate of the realities of the situation.

C *A word should be said about the position of Britain and France, for the former claimed a high degree of independence by virtue of her possession of the 'megaton weapon', and the latter had already caused some embarrassment to the western allies by the atomic tests she continued to hold during the voluntary moratorium:*

1 On April 15th, 1960 (Good Friday), some twenty thousand people in Great Britain marched from the nuclear research establishment at Aldermaston to London. As members of an organisation called the 'Campaign for Nuclear Disarmament' (CND), they were protesting against British defence policy, and were demanding that Great Britain should take the lead in nuclear disarmament. Their case warranted careful consideration, for it was based upon a practical as well as a moral argument. They stated:

a That Great Britain was indefensible against nuclear attack, and that she would only be safe if she withdrew from NATO, if she refused to let the U.S.A. have bases on her soil, and if she destroyed her nuclear deterrent. If such a policy were carried out, she would be under no threat from Russia, which had no direct quarrel with her.

b There was a great danger that other countries would soon come to possess nuclear bombs, and not only was this dangerous in itself, but they would demand the right to test them and the world would therefore be subject to an ever-increasing dose of radiation. It was the moral duty of Christians, as well as the practical teaching of common sense, to prevent this happening. If the arguments in '*a*' above were accepted, Great Britain was in a unique position to give a lead to the world without sacrificing her own defence interests.

These views caused great trouble within the Labour Party in Great Britain, but have never been accepted by its official leadership, nor by the Conservatives. No one can deny, however, that the CND was, for a decade or more, one of the most powerful pressure groups in British politics. The reason why its views were not more widely accepted was because most British people, like most people in the West as a whole, saw communism as a dynamic force intent upon world domination. Nuclear disarmament might be vital if the world were to survive, but it must be negotiated, controlled, and multi-lateral in application.

There were, however, other voices raised against the doctrine of the 'independent British nuclear deterrent' on the grounds that it was expensive and completely ineffective. The Labour Party leader, Aneurin Bevan, speaking in its favour, pointed out that without it Great Britain would go 'naked' into the conference chamber. But the argument continued, centred around the practical value of an independent British foreign policy in the mid-twentieth century, and upon the truth of Bevan's claim in a world which had altered considerably since his untimely death.

In March 1962, the American Defence Secretary, Mr Robert Macnamara, asserted that the United States nuclear deterrent was alone capable of dealing with any Russian attack, and reports from the U.S.A. claimed that President Kennedy and his military adviser, General Maxwell Taylor, continued to urge Great Britain to scrap her national deterrent in favour of a seaborne nuclear force under NATO control. These reports were, however, never confirmed, and the British Conservative government maintained its defence policy as laid down in the 1957 and 1958 White Papers, though with the reservations imposed upon it by the development of a multi-national NATO force (*see page 28*).

2 The question of disarmament seemed not to be of much significance in French politics under General de Gaulle. Determined to re-create the continental power of France, he not only built his own nuclear weapons and the means of delivering them (e.g. the 'Mirage' bomber, 1963, and Polaris-type submarines, ?1970), but he boycotted disarmament talks, refused to attend the negotiations over Berlin and had, it seemed, little interest in the suspension of nuclear tests. It must be remembered that de Gaulle wished to raise not only France, but Europe under the leadership of France, to a greater place amongst the nations—to the position of a 'Third Force' in the balance of world power.

10 Berlin

A *The birth of the problem:*

1 In 1945, the Grand Alliance—Great Britain, the U.S.A., France and Russia—defeated Germany, but each power was already pursuing selfish ends. Fearing Russia, the West quickly shelved earlier plans for the dismemberment of Germany into small states. Instead, they agreed that each power should administer a zone of Germany until a central German government, acceptable to all the powers, could be set up. (*See map 2 on page 18.*)

2 Berlin, the traditional capital of Germany, was situated 50 miles inside the Russian zone, but it was agreed at Potsdam that, as a symbol of unity (and because neither side would give way), the city should itself be divided into four zones, and administered by the four great powers acting together.

3 It has sometimes been alleged that the Berlin problem arose because of mistakes made in the immediate post-war period, but this is not altogether true, because it was then confidently—if naively—expected that Berlin would soon become the seat of a United Allied Administration for Germany, and then the home of an all-German government. Instead of this, the eastern and western zones of Germany became permanent features and Berlin became the centre of the 'cold war'.

4 The responsibility for the problem must be assessed against the expansionist policies of Stalin at the end of the war, and the latent but ever-present fears of communism which existed in the West. In eastern Europe, Stalin used the Red Army to impose communism upon occupied states. In western Europe, he hoped that communist parties or popular fronts would win control of state governments without

resort to war. Thus the communist parties in France, Italy, Norway, etc. were urged to join coalitions with this in view.

In Germany, the situation was rather complicated because of the immediate and obvious interest which the western allies took in the future of their beaten enemy. Knowing this, Stalin made no immediate attempt to establish a communist party in Germany. For a while, he relied instead upon an anti-fascist alliance, and contented himself by giving key positions in Berlin and East Germany to known communist sympathisers. When Attlee and Truman went to Potsdam in July 1945, however, they were faced with two developments which caused an open split between East and West:

a The Russians had used the three months since the end of the hostilities to organise the government of Berlin in their own interests.

b Stalin had changed his mind in June, and had ordered the setting-up of political parties in Germany.

This meant that Herr Ulbricht's communist party had come into the open and was receiving every support from the Russians. It is fair to say, however, that even at Potsdam there was no question of serious resistance to Russia. The western statesmen, no doubt bearing in mind public opinion in their own countries, and perhaps conscious of Berlin's exposed position within the Russian zone, endeavoured to co-operate with the Russians. This soon proved to be a failure. The Russians indicated that access to the city from the west was to be by one autobahn, one railway and three air-corridors; they refused to supply food to the western sectors of the city, and they encouraged the German communist party to force all Social Democrats into a union with them.

It was, indeed, this last factor which brought matters to a head, because the Germans resisted this move, and the more they did so, the more the West was encouraged to support them. Gradually, almost imperceptibly, the West moved towards a new understanding with the people of Berlin and away from their wartime alliance with the Russian authorities.

5 The first real crisis between the East and the West occurred as a result of the elections that were held in Berlin after pressure from the United States and British governments. In these elections the communist party was heavily defeated and lost all influence in the city assembly. This meant that the Russian Commandant, Kotokov, could no longer dictate to that body, and was therefore forced to work again with the other allied Commandants.

From then on, the Russians did everything possible to obstruct all decisions in the allied meetings, and the West turned even more to consulting the German authorities in private. Western public opinion, however, was still too anti-German to accept an open rift with Russia on this question, and when Kotokov vetoed the election of Ernst Reuter as Mayor of Berlin, the U.S.A. and Great Britain offered no resistance. This, of course, angered the German population of the city, but it also gave them added strength, for Reuter in opposition became a national hero and restored their self-confidence and self-respect.

B *The Berlin blockade:*

1 It is thought that, during 1947, Stalin recognised that no communist government would ever rule over a united Germany until the forces of the U.S.A. had been withdrawn from Europe. It therefore became a major objective of Russian foreign policy to expel the U.S.A. from Europe before a strong western Germany had had sufficient time to develop.

2 The western allies retaliated to this policy at once:

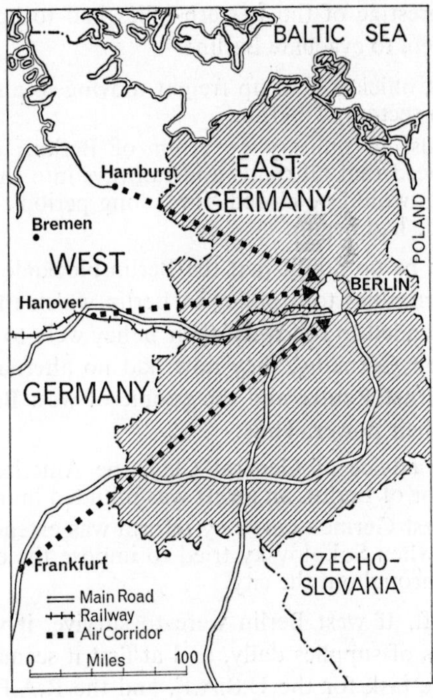

3 The position of Berlin

a They merged the western zones of Germany, both economically and politically.

b They announced the reform of West German currency.

They felt that these two measures, if carried through, would spell disaster to Russian hopes of communist expansion, for they would result in the creation of a prosperous West German state, which would act as an effective buffer in central Europe.

3 From the Russian point of view, this had to be prevented, and the prestige of the western allies had to be ruined by forcing them to evacuate Berlin:

a Russian officials held up freight moving to and from the western sectors of Berlin.

b The Russian military governor of Berlin, Sokolovsky, announced that all roads and railways into the city from the west would be closed 'for a long period'. The Berlin blockade had begun.

4 There can be no doubt that the Berlin blockade committed the western allies to a policy in Berlin which they had not earlier intended to follow. If their policy were to be successful in West Germany, they now had no alternative but to support Ernst Reuter and the people of west Berlin to the limits of their power. Thus:

a On the advice of General Clay, the American military governor of Berlin, an airlift was initiated immediately.

b The West German currency reform was extended to west Berlin when Sokolovsky tried to impose the eastern currency throughout the city.

5 The Airlift. If west Berlin were to survive, it would need 4,000 tons of supplies daily, and at first it seemed to be an impossible task for the U.S.A.F. and the R.A.F. Until the autumn of 1948, Stalin remained confident of success, but from then onwards the air power of the western allies grew at such a rate that in April 1949, in one day alone, a total of 13,000 tons of supplies was flown into the city, and aircraft were landing and taking off at Tempelhof Airport at the rate of one a minute.

6 During the early months of 1949, secret negotiations were begun at the United Nations headquarters, and in April 1949 the blockade was finally lifted. The Grand Alliance was at an end and the division of Germany became an acknowledged fact. Within their respective spheres of influence, East and

West began to build new alliances and to look upon each other with suspicion and open hostility. As this hardening process developed, west Berlin's relations with the West and the presence of Western forces in the city became potential sources of conflict which could be triggered off by the Russian government as and when it suited it.

C *A possible rapprochement following the death of Stalin, March 5th, 1953:*

Malenkov and Beria, the new Russian leaders, may have been willing, largely for domestic reasons, to accept a retreat from East Germany during the spring and summer of 1953, and Sir Winston Churchill, noting their mood, delivered a speech in the House of Commons on May 11th of that year in which he spoke of the possibility of successful negotiations for a permanent settlement in central Europe. In June 1953, the Praesidium in Moscow voted by a small majority in favour of a Russian withdrawal from East Germany, and despite the opposition of Molotov, Kaganovitch and, to some extent, of Khrushchev, it is quite possible that the communist régime of Herr Ulbricht would have been abandoned, had it not been for the East German rising of June 16th–17th. This led the U.S.A. to dissociate herself from Churchill's earlier optimism, whilst in Moscow the opponents of Malenkov and Beria gained the upper hand, and all hope of a successful *détente* was abandoned.

D *The quiet years, 1953–1956:*

These years saw the economic recovery of west Berlin and the growing contrast between conditions there and in the eastern areas of the city. At the same time, the Russian government, hoping to prevent German rearmament, kept up negotiations with the West. No progress was possible, however, for the

West demanded free elections and the right of a sovereign Germany to follow its own foreign policy, thus being free to join NATO if it wished to do so. The Russians, on the other hand, wanted to neutralise Germany and thus provide an area of disengagement in central Europe.

Since then, many British and some American observers have come to believe that at this time, under the American Secretary of State, Mr Foster Dulles, the West was either naive in its statesmanship—for who could blame Russia for refusing to have NATO spread to the borders of Poland, etc?—or unwilling to come to any settlement with Russia, perhaps because of the growing power of the United States' deterrent.

In 1955 a further departure in Russian policy took place, and Bulganin and Khrushchev recognised the Federal German Republic and expected the West to acknowledge the Communist Government of East Germany. This implied that the division of Germany was now accepted as permanent by the East, but the West continued to pay lip-service at least to the ideal of German unification. They refused to recognise the government of Herr Ulbricht and this, more than ever, exposed west Berlin as a western outpost in hostile territory. The dangers inherent in this situation became obvious during the unrest of the following year.

E *The year of the Suez crisis and the Budapest rising—1956:*

In October–November 1956, following a nationalist uprising in Budapest, the Russian troops returned to the city and put down the rebels. At this time, however, relations between the western allies were severely strained because of the Anglo-French intervention at Suez. Thus no united front could be presented to the Russians, and in Berlin, the people who gathered at the Brandenburg Gate or who marched on the Russian Embassy were also incensed against the British and

French for their independent action in the Middle East. Throwing caution to the winds, they might well have committed the West to a third world war, had it not been for a skilful speech by Herr Willy Brandt, the leader of the Social Democrats. Herr Brandt became the Mayor of west Berlin in October 1957, and has played a distinguished and honourable role in world affairs since that date.

F *The crisis of November 1958:*

Possibly owing to domestic pressures, Mr Khrushchev demanded the withdrawal of western troops from Berlin and the recognition of East Germany. He stated that if the West refused these demands, the Russian government would make a separate peace treaty with the East German government and would allow the latter to control the various routes in and out of Berlin. He gave the following May as the final date for such a peace treaty. This placed the West in a difficult position, for if they refused to recognise the rights of East German officials to control their traffic, occasions would soon arise where force would be needed if the routes were to be kept open.

Despite these grave possibilities, the West stood firm: they went about their normal business in the city and waited for Mr Khrushchev to make the first move. This, in fact, did not materialise; instead, it seemed that a general settlement might be possible following the meeting of President Eisenhower and Mr Khrushchev at Camp David. Preparations were made for a Summit Meeting at Paris in May 1960, but before it could take place, the Russians had shot down an American 'U2' 'plane over their territory on a 'spy flight' (*see pages 202–4*).

It is possible that Mr Khrushchev used this episode as an excuse to ruin the conference and place the blame upon the West, for it is known that opposition to a *détente* was again powerful in the Soviet Praesidium, as it had been in 1953. Had the Summit Meeting taken place with negative results, Russia might have been blamed by world opinion, including the neutrals, and this Mr Khrushchev wanted desperately to avoid. This version of the facts appeared in the columns of the western press, but there can be no certainty of its truthfulness. Many people, particularly in Great Britain, whose Prime Minister had worked so hard to prepare for a Summit Meeting, were astonished and angered by the seeming ineptitude of United States' policy in sending the U2 over Russia at that particular time.

G *The events of 1961:*

Though Mr Khrushchev had conceded that no time limit could be set for the settlement of the Berlin problem, the summer of 1961 was to see the world move to the brink of a third world war:

1 In June, Mr Khrushchev and President Kennedy met in Vienna, where once again the Russian leader demanded a settlement to the Berlin problem and the recognition of East Germany.

2 During the months that followed, the number of refugees from East Germany escaping to the West through Berlin rose to an average of 20,000 a month.

The Russians considered west Berlin to be, more than ever, 'a fishbone stuck in our gullet' and Herr Ulbricht's call for support could not go unheeded for much longer. The West, however, had stood firm on this issue since 1958, and Mr Khrushchev had no desire to run the risk of American nuclear intervention. It has therefore been suggested that, though the Berlin Wall, built by the East Germans on August 13th, 1961, to prevent the exodus of refugees from East Germany, was inhuman, it was seen by Mr Khrushchev as a means of preventing war rather than as a direct challenge to Western rights in Berlin.

The immediate danger of war, however, was very great, for the passions of the west Berliners were aroused, not only by the wall which separated families, but also by Herr Ulbricht's policy of organised sabotage on the civilian railway lines to the west and his infuriating demands regarding the checking of allied visitors to East Berlin.

The two heroes of the Berlin crisis at this time were undoubtedly Herr Willy Brandt and President Kennedy's special envoy to Berlin, General Lucius Clay. Whilst Brandt's statesmanlike speeches and firm government of the city kept complete control, General Clay worked on the principle that Mr Khrushchev did not want war. Thus, not only did he send United States' troops into the Russian sector of Berlin after insisting on their right to be there, but he also ordered United States' tanks to take up positions at the crossing point in the Friedrichstrasse.

This show of force, backed by the call-up of United States' reservists and by the knowledge that the U.S.A. was willing to fight rather than retreat from Berlin, saw the West through yet another Berlin crisis.

H *Many solutions to the Berlin problem were put forward:*

1 It was said that Berlin should become an open city, housing United Nations' agencies and protected by United Nations' troops.

2 Some sections of Western opinion felt that the Berlin problem and the division of Germany were results of a war provoked by Hitler and the German people. Thus, any hardships they had to suffer were just retribution for earlier crimes. Placards calling for 'No war over Berlin' were inspired by such anti-German sentiment, which wished to risk nothing on behalf of Germany.

3 Some said that the Berlin problem was essentially part of the larger central European problem, and that it would never be settled until East and West agreed upon a policy for disarmament. Only when fear of attack had been eliminated would there be any chance of German reunification and thus an end to the embarrassment caused by west Berlin's exposed position.

4 There was also a suggestion that the *status quo* should be accepted, that the West should recognise East Germany (a considerable amount of trade was done with her by the nations of the West) and that west Berlin should, for the time being at least, be recognised by the United Nations as a sovereign state in its own right. It would be free to invite friendly nations to station protecting forces within the city, and its relations with foreign states would be conducted by ambassadors in the normal way.

It was thought that the Berlin problem would remain for many years to come. Certain facts, however, became evident from the crises that arose there during the post-war years. It was known that 6,000 American, 3,000 British and 2,000 French troops stationed in the city were useless as a defence force. They functioned purely as a 'trip-wire'. It was also known that Mr Khrushchev, and Stalin before him, both proved that they did not wish to start a war over Berlin. Nevertheless, as long as two opposing régimes face each other in hostility at such close quarters, there is always the possibility of incidents which might themselves lead irrevocably to war.

11 The Hungarian rising and its sequel in Hungary

A *In February 1956, Mr Khrushchev denounced Stalin at the twentieth Communist Party Congress in Moscow, and set in train a series of events which he probably never foresaw:*

In eastern Europe, the new Russian policy of 'destalinisation' led to a widely held belief that states might be allowed to move towards socialism by paths of their own choosing. This, indeed, led to changes of policy from Poland to the Balkans, with perhaps Czechoslovakia and East Germany as the only exceptions. (The latter had bitter memories of her rising in 1953.) In Poland, following serious riots which occurred at Poznan in June, a new economic policy was initiated, and Gomulka, an anti-Stalinist who had been imprisoned earlier, was elected First Secretary of the Party.

A similar pattern of events can be seen in Hungary, where agitation amongst a group of writers and intellectuals developed into a movement which demanded the resignation of Matyas Rakosi, whose repressive policies and subservience to Stalin had earned him universal hatred. It is important to note, however, that the Hungarian movement was, as yet, by no means anti-communist.

Rakosi's fall was succeeded by a struggle for power between Imre Nagy, the new Prime Minister, and Erno Geroe, the new Party Secretary. Nagy undoubtedly wished to take advantage of the new winds which blew from Moscow. At heart he was a Titoist, and on November 1st, thinking that he had defeated his Stalinist rival, he renounced the Warsaw Pact, declared a neutral Hungary and asked the United Nations for assistance.

From this moment on, the nationalism of Hungarians was released: red, white and green flags appeared in the streets and men struggled to overthrow an alien political system which had been imposed from without. This the new Russian leaders could not tolerate, for, had this revolution succeeded, the whole of the Russian political, economic and military position in eastern Europe would have been destroyed, and Mr Khrushchev's supremacy in the Praesidium would have come to an end.

On November 4th, therefore, Russian tanks re-entered Budapest (having withdrawn earlier), and, despite great bravery and last-minute radio appeals to the western allies, the patriots were ruthlessly suppressed.

B *During these events, Nagy took refuge in the Yugoslav legation and was succeeded as Prime Minister by Janos Kadar, whose régime was entrusted by the Russians with the task of resettlement in the years following the October–November risings:*

Kadar was, indeed, an experienced communist leader. He had been imprisoned by the Nazis; he had played some part in the trial of Cardinal Mindszenty in 1948; he had betrayed his former colleague, Laszlo Rajk, when the latter was accused of Titoism in 1949, and he himself had suffered severely at the hands of Rakosi in 1951. For a short while in October 1956, Kadar joined the revolutionaries in Budapest, but he had little enthusiasm for nationalist risings, and when the Russians arrived he was only too pleased to join them. In November, after promising Nagy a safe conduct, Kadar handed him over to the Russians, who deported him to Rumania, where he was later shot. There is, then, little attractive about Janos Kadar, but if justice is to be done, it is necessary to examine the new economic, social and religious policies followed in Hungary by his government since 1956.

C *The consolidation of Kadar's régime was based upon two equally important phenomena:*

1 The physical presence of Russian troops in Hungary:
Until 1959, they were there in considerable numbers, though scattered in small units, for internal security purposes. From

then on, Russian soldiers were seldom seen in public, though it seemed unlikely that Mr Khrushchev would not have made use of any withdrawal, had one taken place. In any case, the Russian frontier is only 160 miles from Budapest, and the Russian Army could return in a matter of hours if it became necessary.

2 Repression and terror:
When Kadar first assumed control of the government, he found it necessary to win time for consolidation by trying to identify himself with the aims of the revolutionaries. On November 10th the government-controlled press stated, 'The Party and the Government regard as sacred and will defend all the achievements which the great national democratic movement, launched on October 23rd, had won.' Moreover, Kadar promised to negotiate the withdrawal of Russian forces, to allow the replacement of the Red Star by the Kossuth Coat of Arms, to abolish compulsory Russian in schools and to purge all Stalinists from the Hungarian Communist Party.

Some people even felt that the revolution had been a success after all, but by the end of November 1956, they had been disillusioned. Then Kadar, who had been re-deploying his regular troops, reorganising his State Security Police and rebuilding his para-military organisations, felt strong enough to come out in his true colours. Nagy was tricked into leaving the Yugoslav Embassy and was abducted by the Russian Police; Summary Courts were set up all over Hungary to deal with 'counter-revolutionaries'; People's Tribunals, reminiscent of those in Paris during Robespierre's ascendancy, were established in Budapest and elsewhere, and a reign of terror ensued which came to its climax with the announcement of the executions of General Maleter and Imre Nagy in the summer of 1958.

Judged from Kadar's point of view, it might have been necessary to eliminate those who might again become the focal points of another revolution. Certainly, from February 1959, when the Minister of Justice announced that the Courts had completed proceedings against counter-revolutionaries, a new calm descended over the country. Amnesty decrees were issued in April 1959 and in March 1960, many internment camps were closed and at least two well-known writers, Tibor Dery and Gyula Hay, were released.

There were, of course, further political trials (e.g. that of Istvan Tabödy in June 1961) but they were to be found in all totalitarian countries at one time or another. They did not indicate any danger of a return to a policy of repression, for it seemed likely that Kadar was now attempting to popularise his régime by providing more consumer goods, as a result of a series of three- and five-year plans designed to increase industrial and agricultural expansion. Indeed, by the mid 1960's Janos Kadar was being given the credit for an improved standard of living and for a relaxation of tension which every Hungarian was beginning to enjoy.

D *To avoid a complete breakdown in the Hungarian economy, Russia and Yugoslavia promised grants in aid and credits amounting to some 1,350 million roubles:*

As a result of this, in May 1957, planning for the future was able to begin again, and by the end of 1960, total industrial output had increased by 40 per cent and the national income as a whole had increased by 20 per cent. Investment plans overtook supplies of capital, however, and they could only be carried out by using up the foreign credits, which had to be repaid between 1961 and 1971, or by increasing the trade deficit which had become apparent by the continued excess of imports over exports.

Despite these difficulties, in 1963 Hungary was engaged upon her latest five-year plan, which anticipated a rise in real wages of some 26–29 per cent and a further rise in the national income of some 55–60 per cent over the 1958 level. Everything depended, once again, upon the ability of the Hungarian worker to achieve his 'norm' or work above it. In the summer of 1961 the government issued a decree stating that labour 'norms' must be kept up to date and 'follow any improvement of the technical conditions of production'. If, through no fault of his own, a Hungarian worker did not fulfil his 'norm' he was likely to have his regular income reduced. There might be more consumer goods in the shops, but only by hard work and good health could they be earned. Moreover, as a member of COMECON (the Council of Mutual Economic Aid, which has been regarded as a Communist Common Market), Hungary was allotted the task of producing bauxite, aluminium products, instruments and telecommunication equipment. Should any part of her five-year plan get into difficulties, there could be no doubt that those products important to the communist bloc as a whole would be given priority and that the standard of living in Hungary would suffer.

E *Collectivisation of agriculture in Hungary:*

This has had a chequered history. From 1953 to 1955, the 'New Course' permitted peasants to leave the 'Producer Co-operatives' and return to private farming, but by October 1956, the Rakosi government had succeeded in forcing most of the peasants back into the 'Co-operatives'. The revolution, of course, freed them once more, and in November 1956 only 8·5 per cent of the arable land belonged to the Collectives.

During 1957 and 1958, the Kadar government did not feel strong enough to force the peasants back to the Producer Co-operatives, but in the autumn of the latter year, the government initiated a slow but subtle policy of aid to the collectivised sector, and denial of all privileges to the private farmers. As a result of this drive, 93·2 per cent of all arable land had returned to collectivisation by March 1961, though many Co-operatives were not yet in production and the peasants were disgruntled. A Hungarian sociological review talked of the 'older peasant generation' being unable to adapt themselves to the 'new socialist policies' and it seemed likely that Kadar's government pinned its faith upon the young who had been educated according to the 'new outlook'.

The results of the first five-year plans, however, indicated that the collectivisation of agriculture met with moderate success, though many Hungarian farmers would still prefer to de-collectivise if they were allowed to do so. To appease them, the state has been making considerable efforts to encourage increased production on the small areas still in private hands.

F *Though such militant church leaders as Mindszenty, Ravasz and Ordasz had been reinstated into their high offices during the revolution, the Roman Catholic and Protestant Churches in Hungary quickly and quietly resumed their passive role in the months that followed the events of November 4th:*

The Hungarian Bench of Bishops and the 'peace priests' (those who actively sponsored the communist peace movement) again combined to establish a form of partnership between church and state similar to that which existed when Rakosi was Prime Minister. Though freedom of worship was acceptable to the state, the church suffered from a series of petty persecutions designed to show who really was sovereign in Hungary, and, to meet this situation, the churches tended to become accommodating and compliant. In April 1959, Archbishop Groesz and other church leaders took the oath of allegiance to the Hungarian Constitution, and soon, any spiritual resistance to communism in Hungary sprang from the simple faith of the older people, for the apparatus of church government had been successfully neutralised.

G *Looking back upon the Hungarian rising in the light of subsequent events, it was possible to reach some conclusions:*

1 Just as the French Revolution of 1789 occurred in a country where the people were not quite so oppressed as they had been, so the Hungarian rising took place during a period of relaxation. The new leadership in Russia had given promise of better times ahead and, indeed, changes had already occurred in Russia.

For students of world affairs, this revolution therefore posed an interesting question. Would it not have been better for eastern Europe, better indeed for the world as a whole, if the Hungarian rising had never occurred? Might not East–West relationships have slowly improved had the Hungarian nationalists not attempted to push Mr Khrushchev too far and too fast? Some observers, particularly from neutralist countries, have shown a degree of sympathy with this point of view. On the other hand, the savage repression carried out by the Russian Army in Budapest on November 4th, 1956, let the world know how determined was the Russian government to maintain its eastern satellite empire—or its *cordon sanitaire*, if it is to be regarded as such.

2 Before the rising, the eastern European peoples had some hope of liberation by the West—particularly those people near middle age who had never taken kindly to the 'new socialist outlook'. From 1956 onwards, however, all hope seemed to have gone. The fall of Budapest taught these peoples that the West would not risk a world war to help them, and consequently, they came to the conclusion that they must make what terms they could with their communist masters. This explains the attitude of the churches,

the peasants, the writers, the workers and the people as a whole. Living standards improved, but communism in eastern Europe was stronger than ever before, though it was Khrushchev's communism, not that of Stalin or Mao Tse-tung.

3 It is interesting to compare Mr Khrushchev's forceful handling of the Hungarian threat with the equally powerful reply given by President Kennedy to the Russian attempt to install Intermediate Range Ballistic Missiles in Cuba in 1962 (*see page 176*). Both Mr Khrushchev and President Kennedy succeeded because, in their own respective spheres, they were supreme in conventional weapons, and they both suspected that the other would not risk nuclear war.

Perhaps both Hungary and Cuba have shown us that, despite any relaxation in the 'cold war' which might come about, it would be foolhardy for either side to interfere in the opponent's sphere of influence. If co-existence is to become a reality, what has still to be settled are the geographical limits of these areas. Certainly this argument strengthens the view that there has been an extension of real-politics (*Real Politik*) in the mid-twentieth century, and that the powers cannot always afford morality in the world of nuclear stalemate.

4 Lastly, the Hungarian rising merely underlined what was already known about the impotence of the United Nations when a great power had no desire to co-operate.

United Nations' resolutions condemning Russia's action in Hungary were passed at the same time as other United Nations' resolutions asking Great Britain to withdraw from Egypt. The fact that Great Britain did withdraw her forces from Egypt was probably due more to the impossible political and strategic position she had got herself into, than to any desire to placate the United Nations. Russia, on the other hand, was in a most sound military position, and political considerations within the communist bloc made it even more necessary for her to remain where she was. In brief, both sides acted for national reasons, and the United Nations probably played little part in their decisions. (*For further notes on the United Nations, see Chapter 25, page 205.*)

12 The growth of communism in the Far East

A *The Moscow Declaration of December 1943 stated the 'need for a democratic and unified China under the Nationalist government' which would assist the other great powers in keeping peace when Germany and Japan were beaten. This was largely the work of the United States' government, since:*

1 Great Britain always disliked the idea of representatives of Nationalist China helping to shape the post-war world alongside the great powers.

2 British business always mistrusted Chiang Kai-shek's government.

The Americans, on the other hand, wished Nationalist China to replace Japan as the large friendly power in the Far East.

B *From August 1945, when Japan surrendered, until December 1949, when Chiang Kai-shek fled to Formosa, a civil war was fought in China between the Nationalists and the Communists under Mao Tse-tung.* (*For details of communism in China, see Chapter 16, page 100*)*:*

The policy of Great Britain and the U.S.A. was to wait and see. Thus:

1 Neither the U.S.A. nor Great Britain responded to Chiang's request for military aid in November 1948.

2 Nor did they reply to his appeal for mediation in January 1949.

3 In April 1949, H.M.S. *Amethyst* was heavily shelled in the Yangtse River.

4 In October 1949, a communist government had been established in Peking.

C *In December 1949, when Chiang Kai-shek fled to Formosa, Great Britain recognised Communist China, because:*

1 India had just done so and Great Britain did not wish to risk the appearance of a split in the Commonwealth.

2 Jurists pointed out that Great Britain traditionally recognised established governments, though this did not imply that she agreed with the particular form of government. (This differed from the United States' attitude: the United States would recognise a government only if it justified itself in their eyes.)

3 Undoubtedly Great Britain feared for her interests in Hong Kong, Shanghai, etc.

4 Great Britain believed that by granting speedy recognition, the gulf between Stalin and Mao Tse-tung might be widened, the latter being induced to look more favourably upon the West. This proved false.

D *In January 1950, there seemed to be some chance that the U.S.A. also would recognise Communist China; indeed, it seemed possible that Chiang Kai-shek might even lose Formosa. Two events put a stop to this:*

1 In February 1950, the Russians signed a thirty-year treaty of friendship with Communist China, followed in April 1950 by a trade treaty.

2 In June 1950, North Korea attacked South Korea, and there began a war which poisoned the relations between the U.S.A. and Communist China.

Throughout 1950, however, Great Britain worked to gain recognition for Communist China, and a seat for her in the Security Council:

1 In September 1950, Great Britain supported a Russian

proposal that Communist China be represented in the Security Council to debate the question of an armed invasion of Formosa.

2 In November 1950, it was on Great Britain's initiative that the Security Council allowed Communist China to be present at the United Nations for General MacArthur's report on Chinese intervention in Korea.

It was only after Great Britain failed to bring the Korean war to a speedy end that her attitude changed. At last, in 1951, Mr Kenneth Younger reported that the government of Great Britain felt that Communist China should not have a seat 'for the time being'.

E *The Korean War—its beginnings:*

1 Since the expulsion of the Japanese, Korea had been administered and occupied by Russia and the U.S.A., their respective zones of occupation being divided along the thirty-eighth parallel. There was no intention at this early date of establishing two separate states in Korea, which had, in fact, a long history of independence as a nation. The Russians, however, wished to establish a communist state in Korea, whilst the Americans were determined to give it a modern democratic constitution.

2 In September 1947, the United Nations sent a temporary commission to Korea, but this was not allowed to enter the Russian zone. (Russia believed that, at that time, the United Nations was dominated by America and her friends.)

3 In May 1948, as a result of a general election held in South Korea, a National Assembly was established, with Syngman Rhee as President. In reply, North Korea set up a People's Democratic Republic under communist control.

4 From 1948 to 1950, the United States government regarded

South Korea as militarily expendable, and both Russia and the U.S.A. withdrew their troops. Russia evacuated North Korea by the end of 1948 and American forces left South Korea by June 1949.

5 Despite threats against each other by the rival Korean governments, the great powers were no longer directly involved, and in January 1950 Mr Acheson, speaking to the National Press Club of America, was able to state that both Korea and Formosa were outside the American defence perimeter.

6 On June 25th, 1950, the armies of North Korea marched south across the thirty-eighth parallel into South Korea.

Thus began a war which was to last until an armistice was signed in July 1953.

7 When the Security Council met at the request of the United States government, it passed a resolution calling for:

(i) A cease-fire.
(ii) The withdrawal of the North Koreans.
(iii) Assistance from all members of the United Nations.

The voting was nine for, one against (Yugoslavia), with no veto from Russia. Their delegate was absent, having walked out earlier as a protest against the United Nations' refusal to give China's seat in the Security Council to Peking and not to Formosa. The Russians later realised what a blunder they had made, and were soon to return to the Security Council.

8 The events of June 27th, 1950:

a Telegrams from the United Nations Committee on Korea (UNCOK) warned that South Korea would fall if immediate help were not given.
b At noon, President Truman gave orders for American air and sea forces to support the South Korean armies.
c In the evening, the Security Council (Russia still absent)

resolved that the United Nations should 'furnish such assistance to the Republic of South Korea as may be necessary to repel the armed attack'.

9 By the end of July 1950, fifty nations had promised assistance to the United Nations. Many democracies felt that, if the aggression in Korea were allowed to pass unchecked, the United Nations Organisation would perish as had the League of Nations in the 1930's. Great Britain also realised that if the western allies did not support the U.S.A. in this matter, the North Atlantic Treaty Organisation had little chance of survival.

10 Comment and criticism:

a Some members of the United Nations believed that North Korea had merely forestalled an imminent attack over the thirty-eighth parallel by South Korea. This argument was refuted by the reports of UNCOK, which declared that North Korean aggression was part of a 'carefully prepared plan'. This is not to say that some members of the South Korean government would not have attacked earlier had the U.S.A. been willing to supply their forces with arms. This the U.S.A. had refused to do.

b It was thought by some that the events in Korea were part of a civil, and not an international, war. There was certainly some truth in this, but it must be remembered that both North and South Korea were organised as separate states and that both had applied to the United Nations for membership.

c Many people thought that the United States' government had taken action on June 27th in anticipation of the Security Council resolution, which was not passed until the evening, thus proving that the United Nations was a vehicle for American policy. There is again some truth in this, but Article 51 of the United Nations Charter expressly states that members have an inherent right to aid a victim of aggression, pending action by the Security Council.

F *The Korean War—its progress:*

1 The British government sent a self-contained force to aid the Americans in July 1950, to be followed in due course by contingents from fourteen other nations.

2 By October 1950, the North Koreans had been pushed back across the thirty-eighth parallel, and the question of advancing into North Korea arose. Those in favour argued that the thirty-eighth parallel had no economic or strategic significance and that the armies of North Korea were still intact. In September 1950, Mr Ernest Bevin had said 'the time has come to unify Korea', but the Chinese government gave a warning that if American forces crossed the thirty-eighth parallel 'China will be forced to intervene'. Mr Anthony Eden, speaking for the opposition in the House of Commons, suggested establishing a boundary across 'the wasp waist of Korea'.

3 On November 5th, 1950, General MacArthur, commanding the United Nations' forces in Korea, first encountered Chinese troops, and on November 25th massive Chinese intervention began. The world seemed to be on the brink of a third world war.

4 Differences grew between the British and the United States governments, especially when U.S. Senators talked of dropping atomic bombs on Manchuria. In December 1950, Mr Attlee visited Washington, but U.S. indignation against Communist China continued to develop, and on February 1st, 1951, the United Nations passed a resolution condemning China as an aggressor. Great Britain supported this resolution half-heartedly, and only provided that the emphasis in future should be on negotiations for peace. It was obvious that, whereas Great Britain wanted a negotiated peace settlement, the United States government demanded punishment: they were intent on building up a new morality.

(*Note:* Arab-Asian proposals for a settlement had been accepted by the Chinese in January, but had met with a poor response in the United States.)

5 By the end of 1950, Chinese forces, using Russian planes and equipment, had pushed the United Nations contingents well back into South Korea, but by April 1951 the front had been established on or near the thirty-eighth parallel. Then began protracted peace negotiations which ended in the armistice of July 1953.

During this time Great Britain and the U.S.A. grew somewhat closer together, because:

(i) Great Britain came to appreciate American difficulties with Syngman Rhee.

(ii) The Chinese charges of 'germ warfare' had been proved false.

(iii) The Americans had exposed the Chinese practice of 'brainwashing' (i.e. persuasion and indoctrination by methods of doubtful morality).

(iv) General MacArthur, who had been in favour of advancing to the Yalu River, had been recalled in April 1951.

6 *a* Throughout this period, the Indian Prime Minister, Mr Nehru, had taken an independent stand. He had publicly criticised the subservience of Peking to Moscow, but he also condemned the United Nations' resolution which had branded China as an aggressor. India was therefore in a position to act as mediator in the negotiations which followed the cease-fire. Nehru made helpful proposals for a compromise which were acceptable to the United Nations but not to the Chinese, in November 1952.

b At the same time, General Eisenhower was elected President of the United States, after promising to travel immediately to Korea to bring the war to an end.

c Stalin died on March 5th, 1953, and the consequent relaxation of international tension was noticeable.

As a result of these factors, armistice negotiations were renewed on April 6th, 1953, after an interval of six months. The parties agreed that there should be no compulsory repatriation of prisoners, and the armistice was at last signed at Panmunjon on July 27th, 1953.

G *The Korean War—its results:*

1 United States and Chinese relations were poisoned to such a degree that the atmosphere of mutual suspicion has existed ever since. The 'cold war' had spread to the Far East.

2 The Korean problem was no nearer to solution than it had been when the war started, and though this was discussed at the Geneva Conference of 1954, Korea has remained politically divided ever since along the thirty-eighth parallel.

3 As far as the United Nations Organisation was concerned, the first war of 'collective security' exposed some of its weaknesses. It became obvious that if the United Nations were not to be paralysed by the veto, its Charter would have to be revised. A big step was taken in this direction by the setting up of the 'Uniting for Peace' machinery in November 1950. (*See page 209.*)

4 The West could feel that it had succeeded in containing communism on the Korean front.

5 The Peking government of China could feel happier now that a communist buffer state had been more firmly established on their eastern frontier.

6 The Peking-Moscow axis had been strengthened, and, for some time, China would have to rely upon Russia for her supplies of military equipment. In the early 1950's, this undoubtedly caused satisfaction in Moscow.

7 Anglo-American relations had been somewhat clouded during this period, owing to the British dislike of some

irresponsible statements made by United States Senators, and American suspicion of British motives in the Far East. This mistrust did not quickly dissolve.

Great Britain's relations with the United Nations have varied from year to year, and sometimes from month to month. In 1949, the British government and people warmed to the Organisation, because it was felt that the acrimonious debates in the Security Council had helped to make the U.S.A. alive to the dangers from Soviet Russia. In other words, NATO itself had, to some extent, been conceived at Lake Success. (*See Chapter 25, page 205.*)

At the outbreak of the Korean War, public opinion was quick to appreciate the value of the United Nations as a means of focusing the world's attention upon an act of aggression. It had not been forgotten that Japan, Italy and Germany had made war in the 1930's without fear of retribution. With the League of Nations a 'non-starter' after the immediate withdrawal of the U.S.A., there had been no effective international organisation for peace which could rally public opinion in democratic states. Hitler brought the war upon himself because he aggressed once too often, but several regions of Europe had been overrun by him before he invaded Poland.

Without the United Nations Organisation, the U.S.A. might have resisted the North Korean attack, but she would never have been given such massive support, even though most of it was moral rather than practical.

13 Other significant changes in the Far East during the early post-war years

In the face of the growth of nationalism, the western powers did not follow a common policy.

A *The U.S.A., true to her historical dislike of imperialism, surrendered her sovereignty in the Philippines, though she retained the use of certain military bases in these islands and obtained privileges for her trade:*

This withdrawal on the part of the U.S.A., however, did not bring internal peace to the Philippines, where the extremes of wealth and poverty continued to cause much discontent, particularly when United States aid fell into the hands of the rich and left the poor in a relatively worse position. This situation led to the rise of the National Liberation Forces, pledged to the establishment of social justice in the islands.

B *Great Britain withdrew from India, Burma and Ceylon:*

1 *India* (*see also page 112*) Since the Government of India Act of 1919, which allowed Indians into the Provincial Councils of British India, and the Indian Act of 1933, which gave limited self-government to an all-Indian Federation, the British government had been 'preparing India for self-government'. In 1942 Sir Stafford Cripps had been sent to offer a new constitution, to come into effect after the war, but this had not been acceptable to the Congress Party which demanded nothing short of a British withdrawal. In 1945, the British were willing to accept this, but the situation was complicated by a split in the Indian nationalist movement. The Moslem leader, Jinnah, was demanding a sovereign state of Pakistan for the predominantly Moslem areas of the sub-continent, whilst Nehru, Patel and Gandhi,

Hindu leaders of Congress, still dreamed of a united India, and did not seem disposed to come to an agreement on this issue.

On February 20th, 1947, Mr Attlee announced that Great Britain would transfer power, either to an all-India government, 'or in such other way as may seem more reasonable', not later than June 1948. On June 3rd, 1947, Great Britain proposed a plan for partitioning India, including detailed provisions for seeking the will of the people in areas where the religious communities were closely intermingled. At the same time, Great Britain advanced the date for the transfer of power to August 15th, 1947. By that date, the frontiers had been drawn, and the independent states of Pakistan and India were established. In the six months which followed, some six million people are estimated to have fled from their homes—Moslems seeking refuge in Pakistan and Hindus seeking new lives in India. Often these groups clashed, and in the riots which ensued, many thousands are known to have died.

In Great Britain, some blamed the Labour government for this terrible loss of life, condemning them for being over anxious to dissolve the British Empire. It is well to remember, however, that at that time:

(i) Great Britain was suffering grave financial difficulties and had to reduce her overseas commitments or risk bankruptcy.

(ii) The British government wished to impress upon the U.S.A. that her earlier fear of British imperialism, which had been shown at Yalta, was no longer a valid one.

2 *Ceylon* By the Independence Act of 1947, Ceylon was granted 'fully responsible status within the British Commonwealth'. Great Britain retained the use of the naval base at Trincomalee and, under the leadership of D. S. Senanayake, Ceylon accepted a democratic constitution. The transfer of

power here went very smoothly and, at any rate until 1952, there was little trouble in the new Dominion. It is interesting to note that whereas Pakistan and India were accepted as republics within the Commonwealth, Ceylon did not, during these years, declare herself a republic, but was pleased to pay allegiance to the King as sovereign.

3 *Burma* In a White Paper of May 1945, the British government promised to lead Burma gradually towards self-government within the Commonwealth. It was obvious that this was a long-term policy, and it did not satisfy Burmese nationalism. The Anti-Fascist People's Freedom League, which had a chequered career of collaboration with the Japanese, organised strikes and risings in the populated areas of Burma until, in January 1947, the British government agreed to the election of a Constitutional Assembly. This Assembly resolved to establish an independent republic in Burma, outside the Commonwealth. In October 1947, the British government signed a treaty with Thakin Nu, the Burmese Prime Minister, recognising Burma as an independent sovereign state.

At that time, the troubles which faced it seemed almost insurmountable: there was much banditry; there was organised opposition from the communists; the various races of Burma quarrelled to the point of violence, and the newly elected Burmese government had neither money nor experienced administrators or professional men of any sort at its disposal. Yet somehow Thakin Nu overcame these problems, assisted no doubt by the financial aid he received from the U.S.A., the United Nations and the Colombo Plan.

C *Great Britain did not, however, withdraw from Singapore, Hong Kong, or Malaya:*

The two former colonies were considered to be indispensable

as naval bases for the protection of her interests in the area, and little thought was given to self-government for Malaya in those early days, because:

(i) Apart from the communists in Malaya, there was no nationalist movement among the indigenous population.

(ii) The dollars earned by the sale of Malayan rubber were vital to the reconstruction of post-war Britain. Without them, Great Britain would have had to halve her imports of essential raw materials from the U.S.A.

The British government did, in fact, begin work on a new constitution for Malaya in 1945, but after much discussion, the original plan for a Union of Malay States had to be abandoned in favour of a Federation, which would permit more local autonomy. This came into being in February 1948, and was quickly followed by the outbreak of a rebellion led by communist Chinese living within the Federation. This emergency lasted for five years, and though it was always known that the rebels were a small group, the problems of combating them in such a difficult terrain were so great that, until General Templer was appointed High Commissioner in 1952, there seemed to be no answer to the rebel tactics.

By October 1952, however, General Templer was able to report that the military situation was developing well, and in 1953 there began a gradual relaxation of all emergency measures. General Templer succeeded where others failed because he realised immediately that the rebels could only be put down if they were denied their food supplies. His whole campaign, therefore, was based upon rounding up peasants who might supply the communists with the necessities of life. When this was carried out efficiently, the rebel bands began to come out of the jungle, and the initiative returned to the British.

From 1953–1956, there were further conferences on the future of the Federation, and a year later, in 1957, independence within the Commonwealth was finally achieved. One difficulty which faced those negotiating for the Federation was the relationship between Malaya and Singapore. Because of the large proportion of Chinese to Malays on the island, the Federation had no desire to include it within its boundaries. Finally it was agreed that Singapore should be a self-governing state, and this came into existence in August 1958. As was to be expected, the British insisted upon their rights to the naval base at Singapore; though this was unpopular at the time with the left-wing parties, it seemed to be put on a firmer footing with the establishment of Malaysia in 1963. (*See, however, page 91.*)

D *In countries where other colonialist powers refused to give way to the demands for self-determination, nationalist risings developed into full-scale wars:*

1 *In northern Indo-China*, in the populous areas around Hanoi and Saigon, the forces of the Vietminh, under the communist Ho Chi Minh, began a campaign in December 1946 to expel the French. The latter, however, and especially the French officials on the spot, were quite unwilling to consider withdrawal:

(i) Before the war, they had invested much money in the rice-growing industry of Vietnam, and now they felt entitled to profit from that investment.

(ii) France was intent upon rebuilding her power and prestige after her collapse in 1940. She had already been forced to evacuate Syria, and her position as a great power seemed, to many French people, to depend upon her retention of her other overseas territories.

After the victory of the communists in China, however, the French government was forced to make concessions, and offered terms to Bao Dai, the ex-Emperor of Amman, who had abdicated in 1945. To the Vietnamese, however, Bao Dai appeared to be a puppet, and the fighting continued.

In March 1953, the French and United States' governments issued a joint warning to the Chinese communists, and large quantities of United States' military equipment were sent to Indo-China. Even aircraft, piloted by American crews, were sent, and this caused some bitter criticism from India, who refused them landing rights and condemned the British for allowing them to refuel at the airfields they controlled in Ceylon. In the event all this was in vain: at the Geneva Conference of May 1954 France acknowledged defeat, and Vietnam, Laos and Cambodia became independent, with the area north of the seventeenth parallel falling to communism. This was by no means the end of the story, however, for the communist successes in this area did much to provoke the 'cold war' and the policy of containment in the Far East. (*See Chapters 14 and 15, pages 85 and 92.*)

2 *In the Dutch East Indies*, nationalist risings in Java and Sumatra in 1945 had been assisted by the retreating Japanese, who allowed thousands of rifles and machine-guns to fall into the hands of the Indonesians. These nationalists quickly established a republican government at Djakarta under the leadership of Sukarno, a man who had been imprisoned by the Dutch before the war and who had collaborated with the Japanese during the occupation. The Dutch government, however, refused to recognise this republic, and from November 1946 until December 1949, the Dutch armies fought a losing battle against the nationalists. Then, by The Hague Agreements, Indonesia became independent, though for the time being the Dutch retained western New Guinea, which was of little practical value to them. On May 1st, 1963, this was handed over to Indonesia by the United Nations Organisation, and is now known as West Irian.

E *Only Thailand remained undisturbed by the events of the post-war years:*

Here, nationalist appetites had long been satisfied because Thailand had never been colonised. By skilful diplomacy, the Siamese government always changed sides at the right moment, deserting the Japanese in favour of the advancing British in 1945, and later seeking the protection of the western powers as they pursued their policy of containment against the advance of communism.

The period that has just been discussed saw the emergence of the national principle in the Far East. It had simmered under the power of imperialism since the beginning of the century, in the same way that it did, much earlier, in Europe under the will of Metternich and the Holy Alliance. Just as the revolutions of 1848, however, 'broke the unity of the people throughout Europe' and produced a patchwork quilt of historic and unhistoric nations struggling for survival, so the Second World War loosened the grip of European imperialism overseas and allowed a galaxy of nations to be born or reborn.

Generally speaking, Great Britain managed to release the 'safety valve' in time, and succeeded in retaining most of her ex-colonies within the free association of states which is called the British Commonwealth. Other powers have not played the game with such skill, and in the holocaust, have lost everything, as Metternich did before them.

If, however, imperialism often meant social injustice and the loss of human dignity, it also meant protection and stability. The new states of the Far East, in common with newly emerged states elsewhere, have not only great economic problems to solve, in which they may well play off East against West in the search for the most lucrative agreements, but they may also find themselves in growing conflict with their neighbours as the years go by. Professor Namier said that 1848 started 'the great European war of every nation against its neighbours'. It seems likely that if such a situation is to be avoided in the

Far East, and indeed elsewhere in the world, it will be, for the time being at least, because of the polarisation of the world into two camps, sheltering under the terrible deterrent or agreeing tacitly to peaceful co-existence; or because of the growing effectiveness of the United Nations as a force for peace, even, indeed, as a form of world government.

14 The policy of containment in the Far East

A *It was not until the Japanese attack on Pearl Harbour in December 1941 that the United States government began to make a drastic reappraisal of its defence needs in the Far East:*

Before the Second World War, the U.S.A. had regarded the Pacific Ocean as a natural barrier against her potential enemies in the east, and because of this, had often refused to vote the funds necessary for the creation of an adequate defence line, though more bases were in fact established between 1936 and 1941.

In 1950, however, before the Korean war began, and long before the collapse of French power in Indo-China, Mr Dean Acheson, the United States Secretary for Defence, spoke of the necessity of building a 'defensive perimeter' ranging from the Aleutians, through Japan, Okinawa and Guam to the Philippines. At that time, however, the major threat to the U.S.A. was considered to come from Russia, with its bases in the Far East (Petropavlovsk, Nikolaevsk, Komsomolsk and Vladivostok) and its submarine fleets in those waters.

B *Massive intervention by the Communist Chinese in Korea (1950) and the subsequent failure of the United Nations forces to inflict a decisive defeat upon them, led the U.S.A. to strengthen her position in the Pacific:*

1 The immediate threat from Communist China hastened the conclusion of a peace treaty with Japan. General MacArthur began by authorising the Japanese government to establish a National Police Reserve in July 1950, to be trained and equipped by the U.S.A. In September of the following year Japan was recognised as 'a sovereign nation possessing the inherent right of individual and collective self-

defence'. Rearmament was thus permitted and a United States–Japanese Security Pact allowed the U.S.A. to extend her military bases upon the Bonin and Ryukyu Islands and in Japan itself. Japan was now part of the United States 'defensive perimeter'.

2 To quieten Australian and New Zealand fears of a possible revival of Japanese expansionism, and to strengthen her own position in the South Pacific, the United States government, in the same year (1951), concluded the ANZUS Treaty with these countries, guaranteeing them support should they ever be attacked.

3 The U.S.A. also gave more active support to Chiang Kai-shek, and became committed to the idea of 'two Chinas'. Because of this, the island of Formosa assumed a position of great significance in international affairs, as indeed did the islands of Matsu and Quemoy, held by the Chinese Nationalists.

It was sometimes thought that from 1952 to 1958, Mr Foster Dulles, U.S. Secretary of State, Admiral Radford, Chairman of the U.S. Chiefs of Staff, and certain other U.S. Senators were responsible for encouraging Chiang Kai-shek in his belief that United States' forces might be committed to support a Nationalist invasion of the Chinese mainland. This view, which was widely held in Great Britain, tended to bedevil Anglo-American relations during the Presidency of Mr Eisenhower, but, though the United States government concluded a Mutual Defence Treaty with the Chinese Nationalists in February 1955, the defensive nature of this treaty was emphasised when Congress refused to commit U.S. forces to the defence of the 'off-shore' islands, unless it became obvious that a communist attack upon them was only a preliminary to an invasion of Formosa.

This cautious policy was confirmed in 1958, when, in the

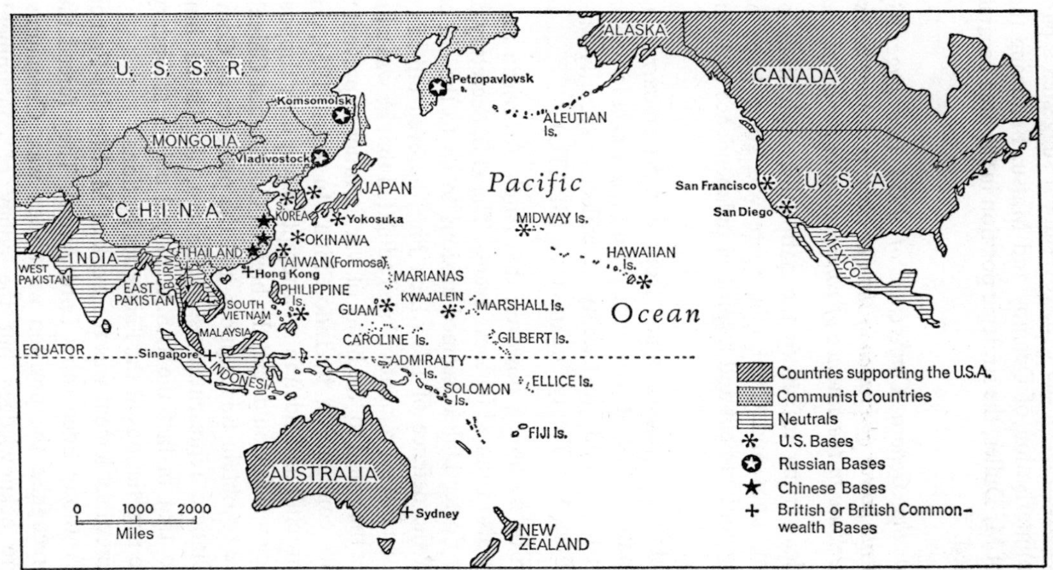

4 The policy of containment in the Far East. The United States wants to strengthen Indonesia as a bulwark against Chinese expansion through South-east Asia, but there has been the problem of Indonesia's opposition to Malaysia.

Sino-American talks, the U.S. government suggested a partial demilitarisation of Quemoy and Matsu. Following the death of Mr Dulles, the strategic position in the area became stabilised.

C *Though the Geneva Conference of 1954 (see page 93) weakened the power of France in the Far East, it did not necessarily contribute to the advance of communism in the area:*

1 By endeavouring to satisfy the nationalist aspirations of Vietnam, Laos and Cambodia, there was some hope of bringing contentment and a spirit of independence to Indo-China.

2 By freeing the western allies from a most embarrassing position in South-east Asia, it enabled them to act in unison to form the second great treaty of collective security—the South-East Asia Treaty Organisation (SEATO).

There can be no doubt, however, that Anglo-American relations were also strained by these events. The U.S. Secretary of State, Mr Foster Dulles, seemed anxious to go to the aid of France in the defence of Dien Bien Phu; he even talked of 'massive and instant retaliation' and admitted that he was willing to take the world to 'the brink of war' in order to prevent a victory for communism in Indo-China. In April 1954, he visited Churchill and Eden in an attempt to win their support for a policy which would 'call the bluff of Communist China'. His failure to obtain this support, and the presence of Communist Chinese representatives at Geneva, displeased him greatly, so that in fact the U.S.A. played only a secondary role in the negotiations at the Palais des Nations.

The Geneva settlement was the work of M. Mendès-France and Mr Anthony Eden (now Lord Avon). They forced the West to recognise the position as it then was. Communist gains were acknowledged but the policy of containment, already adopted in Europe, could now be initiated in the Far East with some hope of success.

D *In September 1954, at a conference in Manila, Mr Dulles was able to persuade Great Britain, France, Australia, New Zealand, Pakistan, Siam and the Philippines to join the U.S.A. in signing the South-East Asia Collective Defence Treaty:*

1 It was based upon the belief that Communist China was aggressive and would, if she could, extend her ideology to all Chinese living in the Far East. There had always been close ties between Chinese living abroad and their homeland; it might be hoped that they would now become missionaries of communism and the new rulers of the indigenous people wherever they lived.

2 Unfortunately, from the Western point of view, not all the peoples of South-east Asia were convinced of the aggressive intentions of either China or Russia.

India, Burma and Indonesia remained neutral and refused the protection offered by the new organisation. It seemed to them to be dominated by western powers, whose interests were only in strengthening their side in the fight against communism. Countries of South-east Asia might benefit from United States' military and financial aid, but only in direct ratio to their value in the 'cold war'. Their hostility to this renewal of Western influence in the Far East is seen in the Bandung Conference, which they organised in April 1955.

E *The United States government soon discovered that the SEATO pact of 1954 was not sufficient for the containment of communism in the Far East:*

Thus, a vast military aid programme was built up in Vietnam and Laos (*pages 92–99*), and major naval and air force bases were established along the 'defensive perimeter' in Guam, Midway, Okinawa, Kwajalein, the Philippines and in Japan. Yokosuka (Japan), for instance, was the only port west of Pearl Harbour (Hawaii) where the U.S.A. could dry-dock her great aircraft-carriers, whilst Okinawa became the headquarters of the U.S. Marine Corps in the Pacific, and of the U.S. Army deployed against the communists in South-east Asia. The refusal of Japan to allow the use of U.S. bases in Japan in the event of a Sino-American war, which arose out of the riots of 1960 and led to the cancellation of President Eisenhower's visit, caused some embarrassment in Washington. With the introduction of Polaris submarines, however, the need for shore bases grew less, and the role of the U.S. ground forces in the Pacific was re-defined as the prevention of internal subversion and the defeat of communist-inspired uprisings.

F *It was hoped that two other developments would contribute to the containment of communism in the Far East:*

1 The U.S.A. made a strenuous effort to win the support of President Sukarno of Indonesia in the struggle against Communist China. To do this, she gave support to Indonesia's claims to Dutch New Guinea, on condition that no further territorial demands would be made. As a result, the United Nations handed Dutch New Guinea (now West Irian) over to Indonesia on May 1st, 1963. The value of Indonesia as an ally of the West was never great, and United States' support for President Sukarno embarrassed not only the Netherlands (a member of NATO) but Australia, New Zealand and Great Britain, which helped to form the Federation of Malaysia, to the north of Indonesia. It should be added, however, that the U.S. government's support for President Sukarno was also intended to help him with the

struggle against the strong communist party within Indonesia itself—a threat never emphasised in Europe but exposed by the unsuccessful communist attempt to overthrow Sukarno in October 1965.

2 The Federation of Malaysia (which consisted of Malaya, Singapore, North Borneo—now Sabah—and Sarawak) was established on September 16th, 1963, after a United Nations investigating team had reported that the inhabitants of Sabah and Sarawak had been adequately consulted.

Despite opposition from Indonesia and from the Philippines, this Federation promised to be both economically prosperous and politically stable. It suffered a setback on September 9th, 1965, when Singapore withdrew to become an independent state, but it still has the active military support of Great Britain, and could develop as a strong anti-communist state at the southern end of the 'defensive perimeter', provided that the people of Sarawak can be successfully assimilated and the disputes with Indonesia and the Philippines settled.

15 Problems in Vietnam and Laos

A *During and after the Second World War, 1939–49:*

1 At the beginning of the war, Vietnam, Cambodia and Laos had been under French rule since 1884. There had been little or no chance for any political development during this period; only the communist party, led by Ho Chi Minh, had been active, working underground against French imperialism. Following an unsuccessful rising in 1930–31, even Ho Chi Minh had to flee to Hong Kong, where he was imprisoned by the British. His movement in Indo-China was broken for the time being, though it revived during the Japanese occupation and attracted to it nationalists of all sorts. The Allies, indeed, made good use of these patriots and supplied them with arms, which were used to good effect against the French later on.

2 At the end of the war, Ho Chi Minh set up a National Liberation Committee which purged the movement of all non-communists, but the country was, once again, occupied by foreign troops—the British south of the sixteenth parallel, and the Chinese to the north of that line. In October 1945, General Leclerc and the French arrived at Saigon to reclaim their colony, but, whilst they were able to assert their authority in the south, the situation remained confused around Hanoi. There, for the time being, the U.S.A. sided with the Vietminh, and undisciplined Chinese soldiers of the Kuomintang murdered and looted in a land where public order had almost broken down.

3 In March 1946 the withdrawal of the Chinese was negotiated, but Ho Chi Minh's relations with the French did not improve. In August he went to France to attend a conference at Fontainebleau on the future of Indo-China, but the

French, in their post-war mood, were unwilling to grant concessions. In December, war between them and the Vietminh began in earnest. This lasted for eight years, and though the French tried to salvage the situation by ruling through the Emperor, Bao Dai, it was always obvious that they intended to retain the real control.

Meanwhile, the Communists had been completely successful in China and were able to assist the Vietminh, who now began to feel confident not only of the eventual political victory, but of a decisive military victory as well.

B *Up to the Geneva Conference of 1954:*

1 The war continued, though by 1953 the losses on both sides had become so great that some compromise seemed essential. The French Prime Minister, M. Laniel, gave some hope of independence within the French Union, and various conferences, both official and unofficial, were held in Vietnam to prepare for negotiations with France. These opened in Paris in 1954, but soon a deadlock was reached, and no solution would have been possible had it not been for Mr Eden's initiative in suggesting a conference at Geneva of French, British, United States' and Russian representatives, to discuss a settlement in the Far East. For this purpose, a conference met on April 26th, 1954, only a few days before the fall of the French garrison at Dien Bien Phu on May 8th. This communist victory strengthened the hand of the Vietminh at the conference table, and eventually, after the new French Prime Minister, M. Mendès-France, had taken charge of the French delegation, a settlement was reached.

2 This settlement divided Vietnam into two parts at the seventeenth parallel. To the north of the line, the Vietminh were recognised as the legal government, whilst the south went to the Nationalist government of Ngo Dinh Diem. Some time

was allowed for the Vietnamese people to travel freely to the zone of their choice, and an unsigned 'Declaration of Intent' added that national elections should be held within two years, in order to re-unite the country. Meanwhile, an International Control Commission of Canadian and Polish members, under the chairmanship of India, was to see that the agreements were being carried out.

C *No settlement in South Vietnam—the fall of Ngo Dinh Diem*:

1 Many years had passed since national elections should have been held, and the Democratic Republic of Vietnam (North Vietnam) soon claimed that the southern government of Ngo Dinh Diem had become the 'fascist puppet' of the United States. South Vietnam was not slow to reply to these charges, pointing out that it had evidence of much subversive activity carried out south of the seventeenth parallel by the 'so-called democratic republic of the north'. These charges and counter-charges contributed to the worsening of relations in Indo-China. In South Vietnam, the communist Viet Cong guerrillas terrorised the countryside.

2 There were several attempts to assassinate Ngo Dinh Diem, including one in February 1962, when his Saigon residence was bombed, and there could be no doubt of his unpopularity, and that of his government, even amongst his own people. Eventually, following repressive measures against the Buddhists, who objected strongly to President Diem's idea of one-party democracy, and the subsequent suspension of U.S. aid, the Vietnamese generals organised a military *coup*, in which President Diem died, but they did not bring about any permanent improvement of the military situation. Indeed, a second *coup* was necessary before General Khanh emerged as the new leader of Vietnam, capable of winning back the support of the U.S.A.

5 Vietnam and Laos

The key to victory in South Vietnam may lie with the peasants. The U.S.A. increased her aid to the new government and sent many 'observers' (troops dressed in civilian clothing) to help stabilise the situation, but it may well be that no successful solution will be found until a strategy similar to that adopted by General Templer in Malaya has had time to bear fruit. In 1963 it was estimated that 500 casualties a day were suffered by those fighting in the guerrilla warfare of South Vietnam, and political reunification was as far away as ever. Indeed, the whole atmosphere had changed since the Geneva Conference of 1954. At that time there were great hopes of an effective *détente* between East and West, but since then, aggressive Chinese propaganda and increased Chinese aid to the Viet Cong have taught statesmen to be more realistic in their ambitions. The governments in Hanoi and Saigon rule over separate states, and though the Control Commission still pays lip-service to the ideal of reunification, it has little hope of success.

For some months the attention of the U.S.A. was concentrated upon bringing peace to the area by the reorganisation of the peasants into 'strategic' or 'new life' hamlets, and by preventing infiltration, not only from the north, but from the state of Laos, whose forests border upon the rich rice-producing areas of South Vietnam. Even these limited ambitions, however, were never achieved, and in August 1964 North Vietnamese torpedo boats attacked U.S. destroyers in the Gulf of Tongking. After some hesitation the U.S. government retaliated by bombing naval bases in North Vietnam, and thus began a new and controversial departure in U.S. policy. For some weeks after the bombing attacks, the Viet Cong ceased military operations south of the 17th parallel, but in October they began again with renewed intensity. Indeed, the situation in South Vietnam deteriorated so much at this time, with General Khanh giving way—at least temporarily—to Trou van Huong and an interim government, that President Johnson (newly returned in the U.S. Presidential elections) decided to commit large numbers of U.S. troops in support of the South Vietnamese and to embark upon a whole series of bombing raids on Hanoi and other military installations in the north.

Left-wing and liberal opinion in the West has been very critical of this new U.S. policy, but President Johnson received loyal support throughout 1965 from a new Labour government in Britain and from most of his SEATO partners. Nonetheless it would be well to remember that, sitting in the wings, President de Gaulle suggested, as the only practical solution, the neutralisation of all south-east Asia; but such a policy could never be implemented until a cease-fire were arranged and the integrity of the area were again guaranteed by the Great Powers. This would require a withdrawal of the Viet Cong from South Vietnam as part of any general settlement to which the U.S.A. could agree.

D *The problem of Laos:*

1 At Geneva in 1954, the neutralisation of Laos and Cambodia was to be an integral part of the South-east Asian settlement. If that area was to have any chance of settling down when the French had withdrawn, there must be no interference from outside. In Cambodia, the government of Prince Sihanouk was strong enough and popular enough to suppress the communist minority, thus providing time for the new state to overcome its early difficulties. In Laos, however, the Pathet Lao communists, greatly helped by the Vietminh from North Vietnam, soon took control of the forests of northern Laos, whilst communist propaganda was intensified, preventing any chance of reconciliation amongst the non-communist elements. The Geneva Agreement of 1954 provided for the withdrawal of all foreign troops from Laos and for a political settlement, which, after much heart-searching, was reached at Vientiane in 1957.

2 The failure of this settlement was inevitable, however, for the Pathet Lao were joined by the rebel Captain Kong Lee, and the communists strengthened their positions in the north and even organised an airlift to bring in arms from Hanoi. To all this, the royal government of Laos replied by requesting arms from the U.S.A. Though the United States denied giving arms 'which they had not before', there can be little doubt that an explosive situation was developing in 1961–62, when the co-chairmen of the Geneva Conference (i.e. the British and Russian Foreign Ministers) convened another meeting to discuss the problems of Laos. This conference almost came to grief at once, when it seemed unlikely that a Laotian government, adequately representative of the people, could be formed. Eventually, however, this difficulty was overcome when the neutralist Prince Souvanna Phouma accepted office as Prime Minister, over a cabinet which contained both right-wing and left-wing elements. On the 23rd July, 1962, the text of an agreement was published, which provided that the government would:

(i) 'Resolutely apply the five principles of co-existence.'
(ii) 'Forbid any foreign interference in the internal affairs of the kingdom.'
(iii) 'Require the withdrawal from Laos of all foreign troops and military personnel.'
(iv) 'Accept unconditional aid from all countries that wish to help the kingdom of Laos build up an independent and autonomous national economy.'

3 Two major weaknesses soon appeared, however. Because all three contestants for power had to be represented, the Pathet Lao soon found it possible to frustrate all Prince Souvanna Phouma's attempts at government; and they were able to do this because no disciplinary measures could be taken against them. The International Commission proved powerless, and, apart from the fact that Western intervention had

been ruled out by the terms of the Geneva settlement, the right-wing forces of General Phoumi Novasan and the neutralist armies were so undisciplined that the United States government would have been reluctant to offer open military support in any case.

Gradually the situation deteriorated. In April 1963, the Pathet Lao leaders left the capital, Vientiane, claiming that the presence of right-wing troops in the city made it unsafe for them, and a year later, in April 1964, an army *coup d'état*, though it eventually left Prince Souvanna Phouma still in command of the government, finally destroyed the idea of neutralism which had been conceived at Geneva in 1962. This right-wing *coup* was certainly not engineered by the United States government, but the Pathet Lao used it as an excuse to open a further successful military offensive. If this should prove decisive, and Laos should be overrun by the Communists, Ho Chi Minh's route to the Viet Cong would be open and—perhaps even more disastrous for the West—Communist control of the Mekong River valley would open the way through neighbouring Cambodia and Thailand to the rich rice-growing areas of Malaysia and Burma. Undoubtedly this had been in the mind of the U.S. government when, in May 1963, the first American troops landed in Cambodia at Udon and defensive agreements were concluded with the government of Thailand, which would allow the effective deployment of SEATO forces in defence of that area if the occasion should arise.

16 Communist China

A *China in the nineteenth century:*

The history of China is punctuated by a number of peasant revolts, but until the rise of Mao Tse-tung, none of them had ever been able to secure the final victory. Moreover, during the nineteenth century a series of corrupt and inefficient governments allowed the West and Tsarist Russia to penetrate deeply into Chinese society. European powers divided the seaboard areas of China into 'spheres of influence'. European traders had the support of their respective navies, and in 1839 the depths of humiliation were plumbed when the debilitating opium trade was freed from the restrictions placed upon it by a weak Chinese administration.

There might have been much to learn from the West at this time about the concept of individualism and the results of applied science, but the Western merchants, bankers and officials grew arrogant and rich, and the Christian missionaries seemed to want to destroy the Chinese faith in Confucianism and Taoism. As the Chinese people grew to hate the West, so they came to despise the Manchu dynasty which allowed such interference.

B *Sun Yat Sen and the Kuomintang:*

The climax came in the Boxer Rising of 1900–1901, when a nationalist movement was put down by a European force which landed at Tientsin and sacked Peking. From that time onward, the end of the Manchu dynasty was in sight. This finally came about in 1911 and was the work of Sun Yat Sen, who intended at that time to found a liberal democracy on Western lines. Dr Sun was proclaimed President of the Chinese Republic, and announced an ambitious programme of reform, which included industrialisation, the end of 'unequal' treaties, and a curbing of the power of the landlords. In fact, however, things did not run smoothly for him and he stood down in favour of Yuan Shih Kai, a former general in the Manchu armies with pretensions to the imperial power. For the moment, it seemed that yet another national rising had failed, but Yuan Shih Kai died in 1916, and the Treaty of Versailles, 1919, by which Japan was given all Germany's territorial and trading rights in China in payment for her assistance in the 1914–1918 war, provoked an indignant response from a united China.

Sun Yat Sen was again returned to power, but this time, instead of looking to the West for guidance, he turned to Russia and to the new philosophy which had been at work there since 1917. Between 1919 and 1925 Dr Sun and his party, the Kuomintang, worked to consolidate their power by force, using Russian weapons and advisers and even working in alliance with known communists.

C *Chiang Kai-shek and the Chinese communists:*

In 1926, a year after Dr Sun's death, a Kuomintang expeditionary force marched north to proclaim the Republic throughout the land. Its leader was Chiang Kai-shek, who had recently returned from training in Russia, and one of its ablest political commissars was Chou en Lai, who was later to become one of the leading statesmen of Communist China. However, as Chiang came nearer to complete dominion over China, he found it impossible to retain his ties with the landlord and business classes at the same time as he maintained the alliance with the communists. Inevitably a choice had to be made, and in 1927, in Shanghai, he began a purge of his left wing. By this action Chiang won the support of the property owners, but to retain it he had to give up all ideas of land reform and rent control. In this lay the seeds of his future downfall.

Meanwhile, surviving communists began to build up their own Soviet State in the hills of Kiangsi. There, they evicted the landlords and rich peasants and developed the idea of collective farming. In 1934, when Chiang tried to surround them, they broke through and, under the leadership of Mao Tse-tung, they set out on their 'Long March'. One hundred thousand began the journey, but by the time they reached Yenan in Shensi (far to the north), only thirty thousand remained to begin again the business of setting up a new Soviet State.

D *Civil war and the Japanese invasion:*

At this time the struggle for power in China was complicated by the Japanese invasion of Manchuria. Instead of uniting his country in the face of a common enemy, Chiang earned the undying hatred of many Chinese by continuing to use the Kuomintang troops against the communists. This policy provoked mutiny amongst his own supporters and gave the communists a great opportunity to pose as the only truly patriotic party. By visiting Chiang amongst his mutinous troops, Chou en Lai was able to bring about a renewal of the Kuomintang-Communist alliance, and for two years, from 1936 to 1938, the Japanese met some semblance of a united front in China.

As the fascist powers of Europe grew in strength, however, Chiang looked more and more to them for assistance. The Germans, Von Siecht and Falkenhausen, became his military advisers, Captain Stenner was put in charge of his bodyguard and a truce with Japan was arranged through the mediation of the Italian Foreign Minister, Count Ciano. By mid-1938, Chiang was in a position to dissolve the alliance with the communists and to renew his attacks upon their stronghold in the north.

E *The Second World War and the triumph of Mao Tse-tung:*

The outbreak of the Second World War made no essential difference to Chiang's policy, for, though he joined the Allies and accepted their war material, his armies continued to avoid action against the Japanese and prepared for the renewal of the civil war against the communists when the time was ripe. This constant inactivity, however, brought corruption into Chiang's administration, and even alienated the merchant and landlord classes, who saw their investments and land overrun by the Japanese. The peasants had long forsaken him, and by 1945 it was obvious that communist influence stretched from the north to the walls of Peking and into the Yangtse Valley. Had it not been for American air support, it is doubtful whether Chiang would ever have kept the coastal plain. As it was, the civil war was fought from 1945 to 1949, to the growing embarrassment of the United States and the gradual realisation throughout the West that Mao Tse-tung and his communist armies would win—not because of Russian help, but because they were well disciplined, dedicated and, most important of all, they had won the support of the Chinese peasants.

F *Communism in China—the growth of communes:*

Though the Communist Party in China had accepted much of Lenin's teaching, and had been pleased to learn from such Russian agents as Voitinsky and Yurin, its leaders had always known that the revolution, when it came, would be based upon the rural population rather than upon the industrial proletariat which orthodoxy demanded. With this in mind, therefore, it is not surprising that Mao Tse-tung insisted upon a policy of gradual socialisation, which would take many years to put into effect.

At first it was necessary to satisfy the land hunger of the peasants by expropriating the landlords. Even this, however, was done in a peculiarly Chinese manner, for instead of the landlords being dethroned by government order, party members moved throughout China urging the peasants themselves to take action. This often led to violence in the early post-war years, especially where a landlord had managed to retain a private army, but it had the significant effect of identifying the people with the policy of the party. It is true that the communist leaders must have known that giving the peasants smallholdings was not likely to solve the problem of poverty. Somehow, more food had to be produced to feed a growing population, many of whom would be needed in the big industrial plants which had to be developed, and in 1949–50 the first move was made towards co-operative farming. This left the land-holding as it had been before, but introduced the idea of mutual aid.

At first, small groups of families were encouraged to pool their resources, then, as the benefits of the system became apparent, the units grew in size until most peasants began to farm to a national plan. By 1956 it was time for the next stage to be introduced. Mutual aid was all very well, but if private ownership remained, it would be difficult to prevent a new 'landlordism' from arising. Mao Tse-tung decided to introduce state collectives in those areas of the north China plain where former Japanese land companies had already developed much of the land and had reclaimed the marshes. Here, the new farm tractors could be put to work and the susceptibilities of the peasants might not be so easily affronted.

It is an old and strong conviction in China that the use of force is an admission of failure, and this may well account for the incessant government advertising which accompanied the setting up of the new 'model co-operatives'. Undoubtedly, the older people found it difficult to adjust themselves to the new social morality, which demanded that the individual should work for the community rather than for himself or his family, but, by 1956, 80–90 per cent of farm lands had been collectivised.

Peasants now became voting members and elected their own managers, most of whom were young, efficient and enthusiastic. Profits were allocated as follows: 10 per cent was re-invested; 20 per cent was shared amongst the peasants in proportion to the amount of land they had contributed to the collective; and 70 per cent was issued in wages, women being paid the same as men.

G *The 'Great Leap Forward':*

The government now concentrated upon an increase in production, and set targets which were to be achieved during the next ten years.

In 1957, because this increase had not kept pace with the needs of the population, and also because the speedy industrialisation, which was held to be 'the key to freedom', had run into difficulties, a period of 'self-criticism' was initiated. Many Chinese intellectuals took the opportunity to question the fundamental purposes of the new régime, but it was soon obvious that the government's wish to 'let a hundred flowers blossom' was intended only to stimulate favourable criticism. Many enemies of the government revealed themselves and were forcibly detained.

As a result of this critical examination of the position, however, and perhaps in spite of it, Mao Tse-tung introduced the revolutionary reforms of 'the Great Leap Forward' in 1958. To him it had now become obvious that only a new type of communised society would solve the problems facing China at that time. People must live collectively, women must be freed from family responsibilities and join the labour force; industry, schools, militia and marketing of produce must all be organised by the communes; there must be a transfer of the labour force from agriculture to industry, and a marriage between mental and manual workers. Everyone must be paid a minimum wage, with bonuses for extraordinary production; food, clothing, housing, education and medicine must be supplied, most of it free, to all. Even burials must be in communal graves, bringing to an end the ancestor worship which was so much a part of the old Chinese society.

It has been said that the communist government of China introduced the communes in 1958 to undermine the family and to eliminate everything to do with the past. In fact, however, this has been greatly exaggerated, particularly in the United States' press. Young married people who have accepted communism still manage to build homes for themselves and their children.

In the Yangchuan mining area of Shansi province, there was a commune which organised the lives of 150,000 people. It included 75 villages, 23 factories or mines, 2 universities, 6 secondary and 22 primary schools, in addition to shops and hospitals. Reports indicated that family life continued there, that the workers enjoyed a security unknown to them before and felt dedicated to a cause which they might not fully understand, but which gave them a feeling of being part of a great experiment. A similar atmosphere was to be found at the Blossoming Hill commune near Wuhan, where much of the labour force had been engaged in the construction of irrigation schemes. Altogether, 4 dams, 85 miles of dykes and a number of pumping stations were built to supply water to arable land that for years had remained largely unproductive. In 1962 the commune had 14,000 members, in 3,500 households. All children attended an elementary school for six years, 600 went on to a low-intermediate school and 30 were sent to the towns for higher education. There was a well-equipped hospital in the commune, several shops, two factories, a quarry and a mechanical workshop for making tools.

It has been pointed out in Russia that this new organisation of society will give the Chinese government an opportunity to discipline the peasants and thus strengthen China's military position. Certainly, life in the communes is methodically planned. Peasants or workers march to the fields or factories singing military songs; they give up some of their spare time to military training and many are allowed to keep their rifles at home. The Chinese magazine *Red Flag* called for the establishment of a nation of 'citizen soldiers', but it might be wrong to conclude from that that Mao Tse-tung in planning foreign aggression. The major enemy in China is still poverty and starvation, and an organisation of society on military lines was designed to increase efficiency in the struggle against nature, as well as to assist the beginnings of large-scale industrialisation.

Despite certain noteworthy exceptions, however, it is already obvious that the commune reform has failed in many parts of China. Capital created in the communes, which should have been ploughed back into them, has too often been invested in the heavy industries of the towns. Farmers who knew nothing of mechanisation have been drafted into factories, and the government was in danger throughout 1960–61 of losing the confidence of the very people upon whom they built their revolution. Mao Tse-tung once said that for new ideas to flourish 'the masses must come to embrace them as their own'. This has not always happened in the experiment of the communes and the 'Great Leap Forward'. Apart from the economic failures, there has also grown up a fear of 'commandism' where orders and discipline have been imposed without consultation.

The Chinese government is now taking stock of the position, and the communisation of society will certainly take much longer than was at first anticipated.

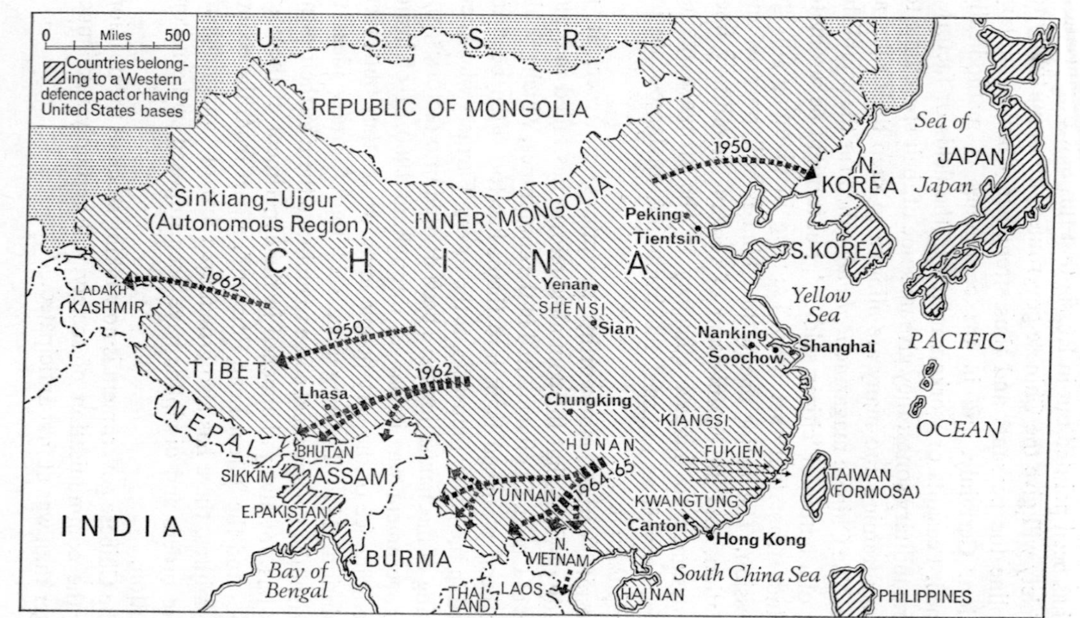

6 Communist China

H *China's foreign policy:*

During the Second World War it was felt, particularly in the U.S.A., that Asia must have a voice in the Grand Alliance. To this end, President Roosevelt insisted that Chiang Kai-shek should be one of the 'Big Four', and he confidently expected post-war China to be a good and grateful friend of the U.S.A. In fact, the communist successes in China not only put an end to this hope but also prepared the way for the Sino-Soviet Treaty of Friendship, Alliance and Mutual Co-existence, which was signed in February 1950. International communism then dominated most of Asia, and had only just been brought to a halt in Europe by the creation of NATO (1949). In the summer of 1950, it made a further effort to expand into South Korea, but found itself up against the armed forces of the U.S.A. and her allies, fighting under the flag of the United Nations. Since then, the Chinese claims on Formosa, and her actions against the off-shore islands of Matsu and Quemoy, have been countered by the continued presence of the American Fleet in the area; whilst her interference in Indo-China has provoked the establishment of SEATO (*see page 89*).

In 1951, the Chinese People's Republic established its undisputed authority over Tibet, and her later occupation of the area drove the Dalai Lama to seek refuge in India. In September 1962, Chinese troops made limited advances across the vaguely defined Sino-Indian frontier, and in November of that year increased the scale of their activity in Ladakh and the North East Frontier Agency. India was unprepared, and for a while it seemed that the Chinese might sweep through into the plains of Assam. However, before Anglo-American aid could have any effect upon the fighting, the Chinese government announced its intention to withdraw to 'the lines of actual control in November 1959'.

In September 1965, it seemed that the Chinese might resume

their attacks against India when the latter was engaged in the war with Pakistan over Kashmir, but, once again, she withdrew following the cease-fire accepted by the belligerents in accordance with the demands of the United Nations.

Two possible explanations of these aggressive actions on the part of China have been advanced by statesmen in the West:

1 One school of thought believed that China had always followed a Trotskyist interpretation of communist doctrine. Her expansionist policies brought millions under communist control, and her repudiation of Mr Khrushchev's idea of 'peaceful co-existence' proved the orthodoxy of her faith and her willingness to face nuclear war rather than modify her policies.

At one time, between 1953 and 1956, it seemed that she would be willing to support the middle-class nationalist movements which were spreading throughout Africa and the Middle East. The agreement with India (1954), the Bandung Conference (1955) and the support given to President Nasser in Egypt, tended to prove that Mao Tse-tung had come to accept Mr Khrushchev's direction. But this, in fact, proved to be a mere interlude, and the Chinese government, perhaps remembering how Russian support for the Kuomintang backfired in 1927 (*see page 101*), soon returned to the belief that encouragement of left-wing revolutionary movements—even to the point of war—was the only policy likely to lead to victory in the end. In this context, her condemnation of Mr Khrushchev's withdrawal from Cuba in October 1962, was easily understandable. Both China and Russia wanted world revolution, but whereas the former was willing to risk world war in order to get it, the latter (then beginning to enjoy a higher standard of living) was not.

2 The second interpretation of China's policy accepted her differences with Mr Khruschchev over peaceful co-existence,

but paid more attention to the domestic problems facing China when considering her as a danger to world peace.

Agricultural production did not guarantee freedom from starvation, industrial output lagged far behind demand, and ignorance and illiteracy continued to bedevil progress. China was still very vulnerable, and, to safeguard her own territories so that the new way of life could develop unhindered, it was necessary to create weak buffer states all around her borders. This was achieved in South-east Asia and North Korea; but along her Tibetan frontier, where she was politically unstable, she was faced by an India whose rejection of military strength allowed her to move ahead of China in industrial and agricultural development. India, therefore, was a menace to China, and this accounted for the attacks of November 1962. If the small frontier states of Nepal, Bhutan and Sikkim could be absorbed into a new buffer state under communist control, the Chinese way of life might be rendered safe from the democratic example of India. Peking may also have had this in mind when she attempted to embarrass India during her war with Pakistan.

Statesmen who followed this line of reasoning did not under-estimate the potential menace of China as a nuclear power, and were not surprised when she exploded her first atomic device in October 1964; but they did not see any real danger from her during the next twenty or thirty years and they advocated her admission into the United Nations in the hope that, as she came more into contact with the world's problems and as her standards of living began to rise, she, too, would reject nuclear war as a means of achieving political ends.

17 India and the Kashmir problem

A *Partition, 1947:*

By the beginning of 1946, the British government had made up its mind to grant independence to India, but the question was—to whom?

The Congress Party claimed to represent all India and demanded a unitary state, but its opponents, the Moslem League, pointed to the solidarity of the ninety million Moslems in India and to the breakdown of the interim government which had been set up in 1946. On February 20th, 1947, Mr Attlee's government declared that India must be prepared to govern herself by June of the following year, and appointed Lord Mountbatten as the last Viceroy to expedite the transfer of power. A month later, in March, the Congress leaders acknowledged the inevitability of partition, but agreement on the areas to be allocated to Pakistan had still to be achieved. This, Lord Mountbatten did with amazing speed. By midsummer he was able to recommend that complete self-government for India and Pakistan should take effect from August of that year, and on June 3rd the British government accepted this recommendation and proceeded to draw up the Indian Independence Act. Partition was not, however, so easily arranged. The Moslems demanded the whole of the Punjab, as well as the whole of Bengal, and their leader, Mohammed Ali Jinnah, put forward a further claim to an 800-mile corridor which would join East and West Pakistan. In the event, the mainly Hindu and Sikh area of the East Punjab joined India, as did West Bengal and Calcutta, which were also predominantly Hindu, but included in Pakistan were the North-west Frontier Province, Baluchistan, Sind, the West Punjab, the Sylhet district of Assam and East and North Bengal.

B *Hyderabad:*

The Indian Independence Act also brought to an end the special relationship which had existed between the Crown and the Indian Princes. They were now to be allowed, in theory at least, to decide their own political future and indeed, had they formed a solid geographical block, they might have been able to set themselves up as a third force in the Indian sub-continent. As it was, their territories were spread far and wide, with the result that Sardar Vallabhai Patel, the member of the Interim Government responsible for the States Department, was able to persuade them to accede to the Indian Union in respect of defence, foreign affairs and communications, whilst retaining their sovereignty in all other matters.

Only two princes resisted the persuasive eloquence of Vallabhai Patel. The Nizam of Hyderabad, though of an indecisive frame of mind, wished to remain independent. He had no wish to join India in becoming a republic, and he pointed to the peculiar traditions and considerable organisation which already existed in his country. Relations between India and Hyderabad soon deteriorated, however. Rioting and other forms of civil disobedience became so prevalent that in September 1948 the Indian government finally settled the matter by the forceful occupation of the territory. Whether they were justified in doing this it is not possible to say, but from the practical point of view there was no other solution in evidence at the time.

C *The Kashmir problem:*

The other state that refused to join the Indian Union was Kashmir, where the Maharajah found himself in a very precarious position. He was a Hindu ruling a largely Moslem state, his government was corrupt, autocratic and reactionary, and, even amongst his own kind, he could find few loyal supporters. In October 1947, as he hesitated, the Moslem tribesmen from the north-west invaded Kashmir and joined their co-religionists against both the Maharajah and the Hindu ruling classes.

This would have complicated the situation in any circumstances, but the widespread massacres of religious minorities in the Punjab had aroused unbelievable bitterness between India and Pakistan. So intense was the hostility between them at this time, that the Indian government immediately concluded that Pakistan had organised the invasion of Kashmir, and, when the Maharajah agreed to join India in return for protection, Union troops were despatched to his assistance with all speed, arriving by air just one day after the formal act of accession.

Opinions differ as to the morality and wisdom of India's action in this event. Some observers felt that had Indian troops not arrived when they did, many Europeans and Hindus would have been massacred, whilst others pointed out that the Maharajah was perfectly free to accede to India if he wished to do so. Critics of India, however, maintain that the majority of the people of Kashmir have always been in favour of accession to Pakistan, and that the Indian government used the tribal invasion from the north-west as an opportunity too good to be missed.

Pakistan felt that her interests were now so deeply challenged that, in early 1948, official detachments of her army were sent to Kashmir, and though neither side wanted a full-scale war to develop, they both began to occupy areas of that country contiguous to their own territories. Finally, the United Nations succeeded in stabilising the position by arranging for a cease-fire to operate from January 1949.

Since 1949 the Kashmir problem has bedevilled Indian-Pakistani relations. It seemed at one time that both sides would agree to abide by the results of a plebiscite, but these

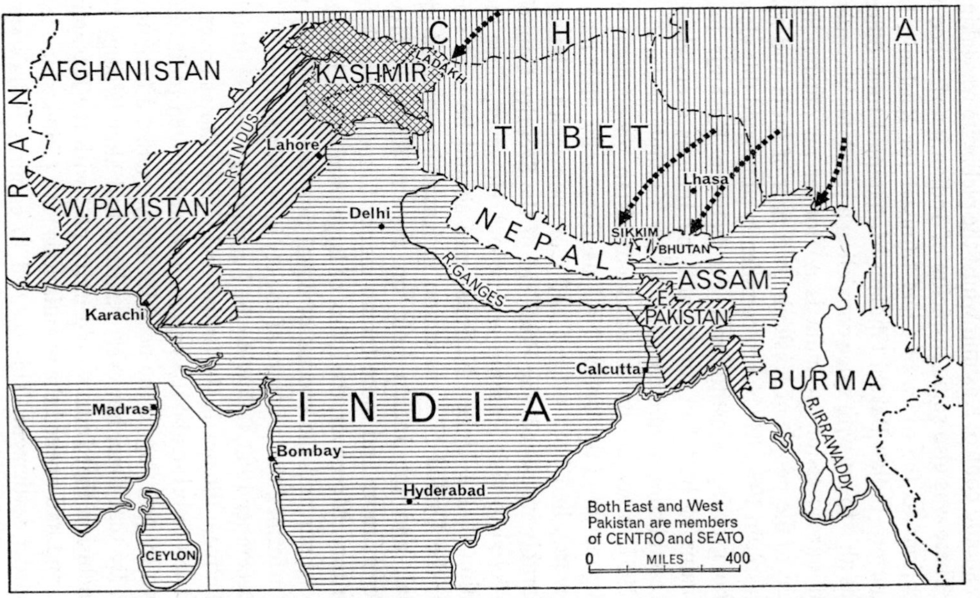

7 India and Pakistan. The dotted line in Kashmir shows the boundary between the areas in Indian possession (to the east) and in Pakistani possession (to the west)

hopes were dashed time after time because of disagreement as to who should control Kashmir whilst the plebiscite was taking place. There was also some suspicion of Indian interference in the elections to the office of Chief Minister for Kashmir. In 1953 the pro-Indian Bakshi Ghulam Mohammed took office, and was able to say with some conviction a year later 'the question of our accession to India is no longer an outstanding problem to the people of Kashmir. It is part of India and will remain so'. In 1956, Mr Nehru confidently supported this view, and the growing constitutional ties between Kashmir and India came to be taken for granted by Indians everywhere.

The establishment of a constitution for Kashmir on January 26th, 1957, however, provoked the Pakistan government to raise the matter at the United Nations. Eventually, after many bitter words had been uttered and Commonwealth relations considerably worsened, the President of the Security Council was ordered to visit Kashmir and report. However, since the suggestion that a United Nations force should be used was vetoed, the United Nations action in Kashmir remained ineffectual, and the Indian hold on eastern Kashmir grew stronger as more and more Indian money found its way into the territory. Moreover, the influx of large numbers of Hindus into Kashmir and the exodus of equal numbers of Moslems has transformed the structure of society in India's favour.

In December 1962, following the humiliating Chinese attack on India from the north, the British and United States governments tried to bring about a *rapprochement* between India and Pakistan by pointing to the need for unity against a common enemy. By that time, however, Pakistan had already come to the conclusion that India would never part with the Kashmir Valley, and had opened the negotiations with China which led to a border settlement. This seemed to confirm India's suspicions of Pakistan, and the well-meaning Anglo-American effort proved valueless. Agreement over Kashmir was as far away as ever, and inevitably India and Pakistan moved nearer and nearer to war.

In June 1965, fighting broke out in the Rann of Kutch and in August Indian troops crossed the cease-fire line to eliminate bases from which, they claimed, hundreds of Pakistanis had begun their infiltration into Indian-held Kashmir. Pakistan denied this and replied with bombardments of Indian positions, and, within days, fighting had broken out along the whole frontier between India and Pakistan. On the world's television screens the intensity of national feeling in both countries was brought home to millions of viewers, whilst the claims and counter-claims of the belligerents were reminiscent of those made in the two world wars.

However, owing to the pressure exercised by the Great Powers acting together through the Security Council of the United Nations, the dangers of a renewed Pakistani–Chinese *entente* were stifled when, in September, Mr Shastri of India and President Ayub Khan of Pakistan reluctantly agreed to a cease-fire. Chinese troops, which had begun to mass on the Sikkim border, were withdrawn, and a Chinese ultimatum to India turned out to be something of a 'paper tiger'.

For some time it seemed that negotiations over Kashmir would not be re-opened for some years, if at all, but, after secretly and meticulously preparing the ground, the Soviet Prime Minister, Mr Kosygin, succeeded in bringing the two sides together at Tashkent in the Soviet republic of Uzbekistan. After some initial difficulties, an historic peace agreement was signed on January 10th, 1966. Not only did both India and Pakistan pledge themselves to foreswear war as a means of settlement in Kashmir, but the Soviet Union became, in effect, the guarantor of Indian and Pakistani frontiers. The significance of this position is not likely to be lost on Communist China.

D *The massacres of 1947:*

Mention has already been made of the terrible massacres which occurred in the Punjab shortly after the transfer of power in 1947. Such was the distribution of population in that territory that, wherever the partition line had been drawn, some two million Sikhs would have been left under Moslem rule. The knowledge that this must happen had sparked off riots in April, which were made worse by the inflammatory speeches of certain Sikh leaders. It has been said that Lord Mountbatten should have arrested these agitators, but, hoping to avoid a large-scale outbreak of civil violence, he refused to do so, though a boundary force of Indian and Pakistani troops under British officers was directed to assist the civil authorities if called upon to do so.

In fact, after August 15th, 1947, violence on an appalling scale broke out, and though it is impossible to apportion blame, it is certain that within hours the most terrible outrages were being committed by both Sikhs and Moslems in nearly every city of the Punjab. The boundary force proved to be completely useless because Indians and Pakistanis refused to co-operate in any action that might demand warlike measures against their co-religionists. As a result it was disbanded, and a series of mass migrations finally brought order out of chaos.

These migrations would have been difficult for even well-established governments to control, but those at New Delhi and Lahore did not yet know what power and personnel they had at their disposal. The railways, for instance, were completely disorganised, and the unusually heavy flooding made matters worse. It was not until November 1957 that the mass movements of population began to decrease (at least temporarily—they continued to flow to and from East Pakistan between 1948 and 1952), but the number of atrocities committed and lives lost could not be accurately estimated.

The difficulties which faced the Indian and Pakistani governments were overwhelming. They had millions of refugees on their hands and little food, clothing or shelter to offer them. It is not surprising that bitterness and suspicion crept into the relations between these two powers, but this was made much worse by the disparity in property left behind by the refugees. In general, the Hindus and Sikhs were better off than the Moslems, and had consequently lost much more. India has been trying to obtain a satisfactory settlement from Pakistan on this issue for many years, but the latter, recognising that any sale of refugee property would benefit India, has shown no desire to treat it as a matter of urgency.

It has been said with some truth that 'If Kashmir is written on the heart of every Pakistani, it is evacuee property which is more apt to make the gorge of Indians rise.' After the passions aroused by the Indo-Pakistani war of 1965 this is difficult to believe.

E *The Indian Constitution:*

The constitution of India is interesting and unique. Written into its preamble, and reflecting the early idealism of its population, is a statement of social and economic policy, the wisdom and practical value of which have been questioned by many students of political theory. The Federal Legislature, and those in the larger states, are bi-cameral; members are elected democratically and they, in turn, act as an electoral college to elect the President of the Union, who appoints all state governors. In theory, the President could govern despotically, but already a convention has grown up which demands that he should act only upon the advice of his ministers. Thus the Indian constitution provides for a constitutional head of state, rather than for an executive figure such as the President of the U.S.A. The Ministers of the Federal government are appointed by the

President, but are responsible to the House of the People, and it is assumed that—as in Great Britain—they will retire in a body if their government suffers defeat in this Assembly. Lastly, the independence of the judiciary is guaranteed, and has been steadily maintained since the withdrawal of British power.

It is true that the continuation of the use of English as the official language of India caused some hard feelings in the decade following independence, but, as the two alternatives, Hindi and Urdu, had become identified with the Hindu and Moslem cultures, it was very difficult to secure agreement on its replacement. By the mid-1960's' however, Hindi had finally been adopted, though English was still used as an 'associate additional language'.

F *India's economic position:*

Economically, India has been moving towards her own form of socialism. Her government has exerted more and more control over private industry, whilst expanding at the same time the public sector. Even so, her economic position has remained weak because she has remained basically 'an agricultural country unable to feed herself'. Primary products still constitute the major part of her exports, and as these are notoriously unstable in world markets, she often finds that she cannot earn sufficient foreign currency to pay for the machine tools and raw materials which her policy of industrialisation demands. She has therefore found herself facing recurring balance-of-payments crises, which foreign loans have only temporarily solved. In common with other developing countries, India requires long-term trading contracts rather than foreign credits for three or four years which merely postpone the day of reckoning.

G *India's foreign policy:*

During the early years of independence, India played a minor role in world affairs, though she developed a warm relationship with Great Britain which has continued off and on ever since. It is true that the British press were most critical of her action in Hyderabad and gave the impression that the British government and people took a pro-Pakistan point of view over the Kashmir affair. It is also true that the Anglo-French invasion of Suez (*pages 142–8*) led to a period of strained relations between New Delhi and London, whilst, since that time, India has voiced her suspicions of the Conservative government's action in the Congo, and kept a watchful eye upon the negotiations for Britain's entry into the Common Market. From the British point of view, further criticisms arose over the annexation of Goa, and distrust of the 'holier than thou' attitude of Mr Krishna Menon was widespread. There was also considerable hostility to the Indian invasion of Pakistan at the outbreak of war in August, 1965. Despite all these difficulties, however, an underlying *entente* has existed between the two countries such as would have been thought impossible, judging from the anti-British speeches of the Congress leaders before independence was granted.

As Indian statesmen have grown more experienced, they have come to pursue a peculiarly Indian foreign policy, which is neutralist, and which—except in relations with Pakistan—seems to be the natural extension into overseas affairs of the Gandhian philosophy of non-violence. It is also indicative of a deep fear of American aggression on the one hand and of Russian dictatorship on the other. For years, Indians saw no danger from China, and were prepared to excuse her invasion of Tibet in 1950. Indeed, in 1954, Mr Nehru recognised Chinese sovereignty over Tibet, and it was thought that the five points of co-existence which appeared in the preamble to the treaty might provide a means of co-existence between the communist and non-communist world. By this time, India was already recognized as an important power in world affairs. Her influence had helped to bring the Korean war to an end, and it was felt by some people that she might now provide an invaluable bridge between East and West—a possible means of preventing a head-on clash of the nuclear powers.

India's neutralism, however, has been shaken by the policy followed by China since 1959. In that year, the Dalai Lama fled to India, and China began her encroachments along India's northern frontier. She laid claims to areas of Ladakh where no recognized frontier existed, and by refusing to accept the MacMahon Line in north-eastern Assam, she threatened Nepal, Sikkim and Bhutan. In 1962 these claims were backed up by a large-scale invasion of Indian territory, which not only exposed the weakness of India's defences, but also brought to an end any remaining trust she had for her Chinese neighbour. Great Britain and the U.S.A. seized the opportunity to try to win India into the Western camp, and Russia was put in the embarrassing position of having to choose between her Chinese partner and her neutralist friend. Whether Russian influence helped to bring about the Chinese withdrawal in the autumn of 1962 is not yet certain; but in any case, India is unlikely to place such reliance upon international morality and high-sounding promises in the future, though it is equally certain that she will not be swept into one of the regional pacts for the containment of communism. Neutralism, perhaps now armed neutralism, remains the basic concept of her foreign policy.

In conclusion, India must be seen against the general background of the Far East. Everywhere, nations are conscious of their poverty and are determined to be rid of it. Whether they will turn to a communist system or prefer the more liberal methods which India has adopted depends upon the relative successes of China and India. Mr Guy Wint summed up the situation exactly when he wrote: 'Whichever country shows the more impressive economic progress, India or China, is likely to be accepted as the social, and perhaps political, leader of Asia.'

All the countries of South-east Asia are watching the competition. At present, though there is plenty of sympathy for communism, the intelligentsia of most of these countries may have a bias in favour of free systems, but they are not indissolubly attached to them. The prime interest is in material advance. If it appears from the result of the test in India and China that, by sacrificing some political freedom, there can be a quicker advance materially, much of the intelligentsia will not hesitate to turn communist. Even in India itself this may happen. If, on the other hand, the progress under the liberal system is striking—if the Colombo Plan achieves its results—there could well be an immense strengthening of the confidence in liberal and democratic ideas. Certainly this may have been encouraged by the appointment of Lal Bahadur Shastri as Prime Minister on the death in 1964 of the revered Pandit Nehru, and also by the added strength given to the Indian government by the Indo-Pakistani war of 1965. Even the tragic death of Mr Shastri the day after the signing of the Tashkent Agreement may have united Indians still further behind their new Prime Minister, Mrs Indira Gandhi, in her efforts to restore good relations with Pakistan, to persuade the U.S. government to sign new Aid Agreements, and to strengthen the Indian economy, so dangerously weakened by drought and famine.

18 The policy of containment in the Near and Middle East

A *There are three major points to bear in mind when considering post-war events in the Near and Middle East:*

1 This was historically an area of Anglo-French influence. The U.S.A. had never had a Middle East policy, and apart from the support she gave to Greece and Turkey (*see page 125*), she showed no desire to become directly involved.

2 It was Arab nationalism, conceived during the First World War, and developing apace after the Second, that proved to be the greatest source of embarrassment to the western powers (*see Chapter 19, page 132*).

3 The policy of containment in the Middle East was not provoked by the advance of communism in the area, as it had been in Europe and in the Far East. It was designed to combat a potential threat rather than a dangerous reality.

B *From 1945 to 1947 there seemed to be some reason to fear either communist expansion or direct Russian aggrandisement at the expense of Greece, Turkey and Iran (Persia):*

1 Hoping to absorb northern Iran into the Soviet Republic of Azerbaijan, the Russians did not withdraw their troops from the area until May 1946.

2 In negotiations with Turkey, the Russian government laid claim to the provinces of Kars and Ardahan, and demanded that the Montreux Agreement of 1936 should be put aside in favour of a Russo-Turkish Treaty, which would allow both governments to share in the control of the Bosporus and Dardanelles. Britain and the U.S.A. joined Turkey in resisting this claim, and the Russians did not press it further.

3 In December 1944, British forces put down a communist rising in Athens, but, once communist governments had been established in Yugoslavia, Bulgaria and Albania, there was every chance that the Greek communists would succeed in overthrowing the democratic government in Athens, a régime which depended upon British military and financial assistance for its survival. In February 1947, however, Great Britain warned the U.S.A. that such was the state of her own economy, she would be unable to assist the Greek government after the end of March that year. On March 12th President Truman asked Congress to vote four hundred million dollars as aid to Greece and Turkey. There can be no doubt that this not only saved Greece from communism, but it improved morale in Turkey and prepared the way for both countries to enter NATO in 1952.

C *The collective defence of the Near East was further strengthened in June 1949, when Yugoslavia was expelled from the Cominform, because:*

1 By September 1949, the Greek civil war was over, and slowly and tentatively Yugoslavia, Greece and Turkey felt their way towards a Treaty of Friendship in February 1953, and a defensive alliance, known as the Balkan Pact, in August 1954.

2 Yugoslavia remained hostile to Russia from 1949 to 1955, when Mr Khrushchev succeeded in reaching an understanding with Marshal Tito. During this period Tito accepted aid from the West, yet retained the right to criticise both Eastern and Western policy. Yugoslavia, in fact, became a neutral in the 'cold war', with the result that the Balkan Pact has never taken its place as part of the Western shield against aggressive communism.

D *Other attempts were made to form a collective defence treaty for the Middle East:*

1 In 1951 Great Britain, France and Turkey tried, unsuccessfully, to arouse enthusiasm amongst the Arab nations for a Middle East Defence Organisation.

2 In 1953 Mr Dulles, the U.S. Secretary of State, suggested that such a pact should be made, though he showed no desire for the U.S.A. to be included in it, and the idea was not immediately followed up.

3 The Baghdad Pact of October 1955 grew from small beginnings:

a In February 1954, Turkey and Pakistan made a Defence Treaty.

b In December 1954, when Iraq announced that she was about to end the Anglo-Iraqi Treaty, Great Britain realised that if her interests were to be protected in the area, it would have to be on a multi-lateral basis. She therefore began to prepare the way for such an arrangement.

c In January 1955, Iraq opened negotiations with Turkey. Great Britain joined in March, Pakistan in September, and the alliance was completed with the admission of Iran in October.

The Baghdad Pact was received with enthusiasm only in those countries which were exposed to any immediate acts of aggression by Russia. In Iraq it was extremely unpopular, and there were outspoken criticisms of it in the newspapers. Nuri es Said, the Prime Minister, succeeded in restoring order in the streets only by using very firm police measures. Elsewhere in the Arab world, and particularly in Egypt, it was condemned as 'an agent of Western imperialism' and as an obstacle to Arab unity.

E *From 1956, after the Suez crisis (pages 142–8), the U.S.A. was forced—however reluctantly—to play a powerful role in the Middle East:*

1 In November 1956, the United States government declared that it would support the independence of the Baghdad Pact powers, and actually joined the Military Committee of the pact in 1957, though the U.S.A. did not become a member.

2 On March 5th, 1957, the United States Senate agreed that U.S. forces might be used by the President against 'overt armed aggression from any nation controlled by international communism'. Military and economic aid was also promised to those states who required it in the fight against communism. This was called the 'Eisenhower Doctrine'. It is doubtful whether it had much effect upon the situation generally, though some states (Jordan) accepted it, whilst others (Egypt) repudiated it. It was followed immediately, however, by an abortive proposal from the Russian government that there should be a Joint Four-Power Declaration on the Middle East—each power promising to refrain from supplying arms to the area.

F *The defection of Iraq:*

1 On July 14th, 1958, King Feisal of Iraq, his uncle, Crown Prince Ilahi and the pro-British Prime Minister, Nuri es Said, were murdered in a revolution which ended with the proclamation of an Iraqi Republic, led by Brigadier Abdul el Kassim.

2 The U.S.A. saw in this revolution 'indirect aggression' by Russia, and on the following day, July 15th, President Eisenhower ordered United States Marines to land in the Lebanon from the American Sixth Fleet, which had been patrolling the eastern Mediterranean for some time. This action was

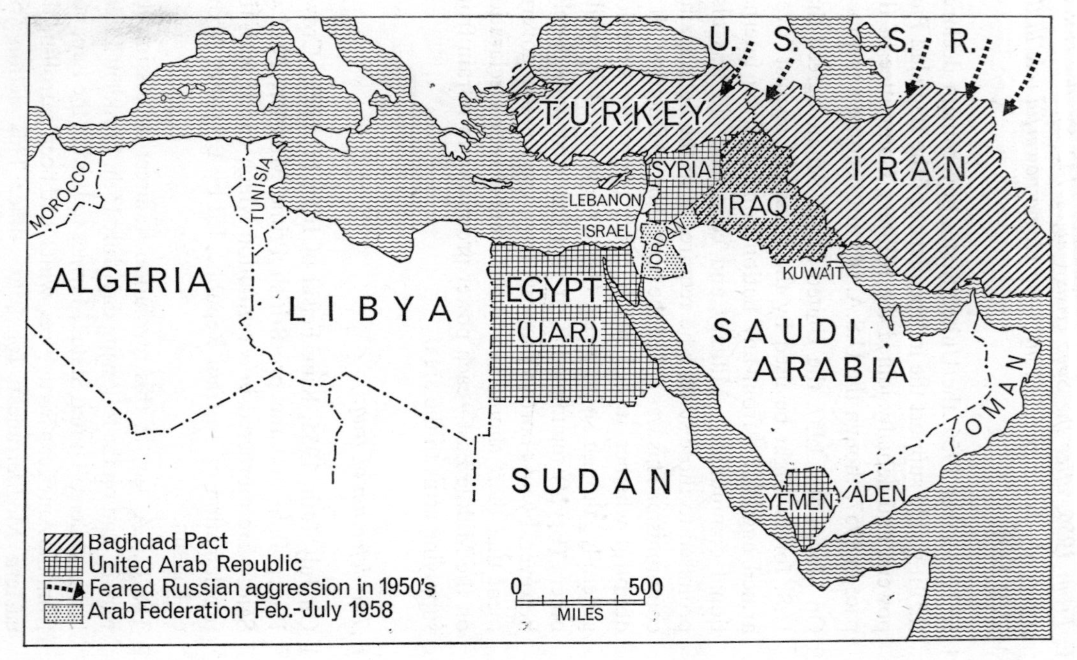
U. S. S. R.
TURKEY
IRAN
SYRIA
IRAQ
LEBANON
ISRAEL
JORDAN
KUWAIT
EGYPT
(U.A.R.)
SAUDI
ARABIA
OMAN
YEMEN
ADEN
SUDAN
LIBYA
ALGERIA
TUNISIA
MOROCCO
Baghdad Pact
United Arab Republic
Feared Russian aggression in 1950's
Arab Federation Feb.-July 1958
0
500
MILES

approved by the remaining members of the Baghdad Pact, but it was, of course, denounced by the Russian government. After a visit to Moscow, President Nasser also denounced the United States' intervention.

3 On July 17th the British government, fearing that a similar rebellion might now occur in Jordan, ordered British airborne troops to land in that country from Cyprus.

The presence of the British and United States forces in the Middle East probably had a calming effect upon the area at that time, for there were no further rebellions, whether communist-inspired or not. Any hope, however, of a successful counter-revolution being launched in Iraq was also proved out of the question, and at the August meeting of the Baghdad Pact Council in London, the western powers, Turkey, Iran and Pakistan, decided to recognise the new Republic of Iraq.

Strange as it may seem, General Kassim did not immediately denounce the Baghdad Pact, and it was not until 1959 that Iraq finally withdrew from it. Since then it has been known as the Central Treaty Organisation, and, because its members have

---

opposite:

8 The Middle East: areas of crisis in the 1950's

a The Baghdad Pact (October 1955) includes Turkey, Iraq, Iran (Persia), Great Britain and Pakistan.

b The United Arab Republic was formed by Egypt and Syria in February 1958. In March the Yemen joined the U.A.R. in a federation known as the United Arab States. The federation was broken up on Syria's withdrawal from the U.A.R. in 1961.

c In February 1958 Jordan and Iraq formed the ill-fated Arab Federation, which was the Hashemite attempt to counter the power of the U.A.R. in the Middle East.

apparently come to believe that left-wing Arab nationalism is essentially neutralist and not necessarily communist, their relations with the remainder of the Arab world have improved.

G *It was in the spring of 1955, at the time of the Bandung Conference, that Russian policy in the Middle East underwent a change of the greatest significance:*

1 Until this time, Moscow had always been most cautious in its relations with Arab nationalism. Marxist ideology demanded the creation of a communist party which could be the only instrument capable of carrying through a successful revolution. The nationalist leaders of the Middle East were middle-class men, and therefore potential traitors to the revolution because they would be content with 'formal independence'.

After the death of Stalin in 1953, this attitude softened considerably, when it was realised that the common enemy was western imperialism; but it was not until after the Twentieth Communist Party Congress that Mr Khrushchev came to believe that the achievement of world communism would be a slow and complicated process. The simple dialectic of Marx and Lenin had to be adapted to the balance of forces in the mid-twentieth century, and, if communism were ultimately to triumph, it would, for the time being, have to accept—and even to assist in—the birth of a third force or neutral bloc. Mr Khrushchev was confident that, in the end, the newly independent states would collapse under the burden of social and economic difficulties. When that happened, the masses would turn against their bourgeois leaders and the time would be ripe for a further advance of communism, but patience was necessary and, in the meantime, every assistance should be given to those who were fighting imperialism in the Middle East.

2 In opposing this new departure in Russian policy, there can be little doubt that the U.S.A. was embarrassed by the history of colonialism which surrounded her allies, whilst the latter were unable satisfactorily to refute the accusations made against them because of their essential oil interests in the Middle East. Great Britain, in particular, tried to solve the problem by working in close liaison with the established régimes. Herein, however, lay the heart of the matter, for new forces were at work in the Middle East: a more sophisticated urban population was developing and some form of education was slowly but surely spreading among the young. Already these students were predisposed towards the Russians, because it seemed to them that Russia had done more than any other country to defeat fascism, a philosophy which, a decade earlier, had been considered invincible. After 1945, Russian prestige in the Middle East was tremendous. The Russian government was not directly involved (except on the northern borders of such countries as Turkey and Iran, and they were quickly hostile to her) and communist planning, which had industrialised Russia, was acclaimed as the long-awaited remedy for the evils of the backward countries of the Middle East. Industrialisation, indeed, was seen to be the panacea; when achieved, poverty and the inequalities of life would disappear.

When all this is borne in mind, there can be no doubt that Russia did present a threat to the West in the Middle East, but it was not the straightforward threat of open aggression that the West faced in Europe and in the Far East. It is therefore safe to argue that, if the nature of the threat were new, the answer to it should have been something entirely different from a collective security pact, which was designed to meet a normal act of aggression. (*For further notes on this subject, see Chapter 19.*)

19 Politics and nationalism in the Middle East

A *The Eastern question before 1914:*

The policy of containment in the Middle East was complicated by a number of important factors which were not publicly discussed during innumerable crises which arose there in the 1950's. The 'Eastern question' is the name generally given to a problem which has been facing British and European statesmen since William Pitt the Younger realised the significance of Russian expansion towards the Black Sea in the early 1790's. In the beginning, it was the result of three factors which contributed to disturb the balance of power in the area:

1 Since the eighteenth century, the Turkish Empire had been declining in strength.

2 This coincided with the growing power of Russia, whose ambition it has been since the days of Catherine the Great (1762–1796) to control the Dardanelles and Bosporus, and to set up dependent states in the Balkans.

3 Great Britain's interest in the area arose from her desire to protect her trade routes to the Far East and, in particular, her communications with India. Any Russian expansion into the Balkans or her control of the Straits would also threaten British naval supremacy in the eastern Mediterranean.

As British statesmen in the nineteenth century came to realise the significance of the Russian threat, it became British policy to strengthen Turkey against any aggression from the north. In 1854, in partnership with France, Great Britain fought the Crimean War to thwart the ambitions of Nicholas II; and in 1878 at the Congress of Berlin, the Earl of Beaconsfield (Disraeli) forced the Tsar Alexander II to relinquish the gains he had made by the Treaty of San Stephano. It was only when a united Germany, allied to an arrogant Austro-Hungary, temporarily replaced Russia as the main threat to British (and French) interests in the Middle East, that British policy changed to meet the new situation. For the time being, under Kaiser Wilhelm II, Germany assumed—or attempted to assume—the role of protector of Turkey. Trade links overland between central Europe and the Middle East began to threaten Anglo-French economic interests in the area, and helped to bring about a *rapprochement* with Russia before the First World War.

B *The First World War and its consequences:*

As a result of this war, other and more revolutionary changes occurred in the balance of power in the area. Not only was the German-Turkish partnership broken up, but the whole of the Ottoman Empire disintegrated before the British-inspired nationalism of the Arabs. Moreover, for some time to come, the menace of Russian ambition was removed from the scene by the Bolshevik Revolution in the October of 1917, and Great Britain and France were left alone, free to shape events in their own interests. The Middle East was now more valuable than ever to them, for not only was it the bridgehead to India and Asia, but it was about to become the world's greatest source of oil. Thus, Arab nationalism had to be kept under control, and the many conflicting promises and pledges which had been made during the war had somehow to be settled or quietly forgotten. These included:

(i) The British arrangements with King Hussein of the Hejaz and with Ibn Saud of the Wahabbis.

(ii) The MacMahon Pledge to the Arabs, 1916.

(iii) The Sykes-Picot Agreement regarding the post-war settlement of the area, 1916.

(iv) The Balfour Declaration promising a national home for the Jewish people, 1917.

(v) The Treaty of London, which gave Italy some hopes of compensation in the Middle East, 1915.

(vi) The claims of the Greek Prime Minister, M. Venizelos, which were at one time supported by the British Premier, Lloyd George.

C *The inter-war period:*

In the event, none of the Middle Eastern states gained their independence on the withdrawal of Turkish suzerainty, for into the vacuum moved the two imperial powers, France and Great Britain. Their purpose was not only to further their own economic interests in the area, but in many cases, to carry out the mandate of the League of Nations and to lead the new Arab states towards self-government. There were, of course, grave complications:

1 The fact that Franco-British economic interests in the Middle East were so extensive led to a mistrust of all their motives. They did bring education, roads, railways, medicine, etc. to the lands under their guidance, but they received little thanks because these innovations were always accompanied by certain political, military or economic demands, which offended against the dignity at least of those Arabs who had become urbanised in the changing society.

2 In Palestine, the entry of large numbers of Jews and the growing industrialisation of the country led to revolts (1929 and 1936) and to a Royal Commission, which suggested partition. This neither Arabs nor Jews would accept.

3 In Egypt, which had a tradition of independence from the days of Mahomet Ali (1830's) and which never was mandated territory, Great Britain continued to work for the establishment of a sovereign, but friendly, state. This design,

however, was always thwarted by the demands of the Empire, which included the needs of global defence and the protection of economic interests in the Sudan as well as in Egypt. Nevertheless, between 1922 and 1939, the Egyptians won a certain degree of independence, though the Palace government of King Fuad remained intensely unpopular with the people, and the 1923 Constitution was never put into effect.

During the 1930's, the discontented elements in the Middle East, mostly the partially educated and some of the commercial classes, found a cause for hope in the growth of fascism. In 1940–1941, Raschid Ali almost overthrew the pro-Allied government of Iraq, and numbers of fascist sympathisers were to be found in Syria, Egypt and elsewhere.

D *The Second World War and after:*

During the Second World War, Turkey was enabled to maintain her neutrality, and friendly governments remained in control of the Arab states because the British Eighth Army prevented any Italian or German penetration from Libya, and the Russians destroyed any German hopes of an invasion from the north by their gallant defence of Stalingrad.

In fact, of course, the *status quo* had not been preserved in the Middle East—new forces were at work which caused Great Britain and France to take stock of their new position in the post-war world and allowed the frustrated nationalism of the Arabs (and Jews) to burst forth with all the hopes and extravagances of those inexperienced in world diplomacy.

To add to the complexities of this situation, there arose on one hand the new state of Israel, backed by U.S. money and recognised by the United Nations, and, on the other, a new appreciation of Russia, which had borne the lion's share of the land fighting against Germany, which had no embarrassing past to live down in the Middle East, and whose communist system seemed to offer the panacea of industrialisation in the quickest possible time.

Superficially, it seems incredible that the Russian government did not play a more active part in the Middle East during the immediate post-war years, but this can be understood if we remember the great gains that Russia had to consolidate in Europe and in the Balkans, and if we recognise the orthodoxy of Russian communism during the Stalinist era. It was then felt that no great progress could be made in the Middle East until the Arab states had expelled their imperial overlords and overthrown their feudal dynasties. Even then, the resultant supremacy of the bourgeoisie in the Middle East would be nationalistic, capitalist and transitory. Its very nature would be hostile to international communism and a further revolution of the proletariat would be necessary before Russia could expect any success there. Moreover, Bolshevik ethics tended to teach that communist expansion could only follow a period of patient and difficult preparation. Thus, during the first post-war decade, communist party organisations were built up (sometimes underground) and the state of Israel was recognised, because it was felt that this would embarrass the British-controlled Arab League; but no official attempts were made to support the new nationalist leaders, who were regarded in those days as 'potential traitors'.

It was not until the new policies of Khrushchev and Shepilov were introduced in 1955 that Russia entered the lists as a serious threat in the Middle East. It was then that the communist philosophers and policy-makers came to accept the middle-class nationalism of the Arab states, and their proclaimed adherence to neutralism, as quasi-permanent features of the mid-twentieth century. Instead of trying to undermine them from within, Russia now offered them financial or military aid in an all-out effort to win their support. By accepting their primary products at prices above the level of world markets, there would also be some hope that they would become economically dependent upon Russia, a danger which Marshal Tito of Yugoslavia and later Colonel Nasser of Egypt were not slow to realise. In any case, it was now felt in Moscow that even if the neutrals remained as a 'third force' in the world, they would certainly not fall under Western influence, and only time was needed before they came inevitably to accept the communist faith.

Such then, was the background to the events which brought the Middle East to the centre of the world's stage in the 1950's.

E *The establishment of Israel:*

Since 1919 Great Britain had been responsible for the government of Palestine as a mandated territory of the League of Nations. After the defeat of Nazi Germany in 1945, the question of Jewish immigration, which had assumed worrying proportions in the 1930's, now presented the British government with an unanswerable problem.

Though earlier in the century Palestine had been 90 per cent Arab, Nazi persecution of the Jews had been so inhuman that world opinion (and in particular public opinion in the U.S.A.) demanded that a national home should be found for them. Thirty-eight of the forty-eight American states, indeed, petitioned President Truman to help make this effective. In trying to control illegal immigration and deal justly with Jew and Arab alike, Mr Ernest Bevin, the British Foreign Secretary, became one of the most unpopular men in the world.

Finally, in November 1947, after a United Nations' scheme for partition had been rejected by the Arabs, the British government announced that they intended to surrender the mandate and withdraw from the area. There was an immediate meeting of the Arab League, initiated by the government of

Egypt, to discuss a plan for the rescue of Palestine from Jewish hands, but only Jordan had an army strong enough (the British-controlled Arab Legion). On May 15th, 1948, the day after the Republic of Israel had been proclaimed, Jordan's army led an Arab invasion of Palestine in an effort to occupy the Arab-populated regions. Mr Ernest Bevin seems to have given his blessing to the venture though with the *caveat*, 'don't go occupying areas allotted to the Jews'.

During the following months, the lack of political unity in the Arab world became as apparent as the inefficiency of their armies. After an armistice had been concluded at Rhodes in February 1949, the Israelis initiated separate talks with King Abdullah of Jordan. Though their demands were harsh, Abdullah accepted them, thus doubling his own subject population but losing the respect and friendship of the other Arab states. It is not surprising that he was assassinated in 1951.

Two points of interest are worth noting as a result of this first crisis in post-war Middle Eastern affairs:

(i) Anglo-American relations became strained when the United States seemed so ready to criticise British policy, yet refused to involve herself officially in the area. The British did not forget this in 1956 at the time of 'Suez'.

(ii) The failure of the Arab armies in 1948–49 and the lack of Arab unity had a great effect upon young officers such as Colonel Nasser who, with General Neguib, began to prepare the *coup d'état* which was to overthrow King Farouk in 1952.

F *The Anglo-Iranian Oil dispute, 1951:*

In April 1951, under the leadership of Dr Mussadiq, the Iranian Majlis (Parliament) revoked the concession which it had made to the Anglo-Iranian Oil Company (AIOC) in 1933, by passing a bill for the nationalisation of the industry. On May 26th, 1951, the British government acted on behalf of the AIOC by

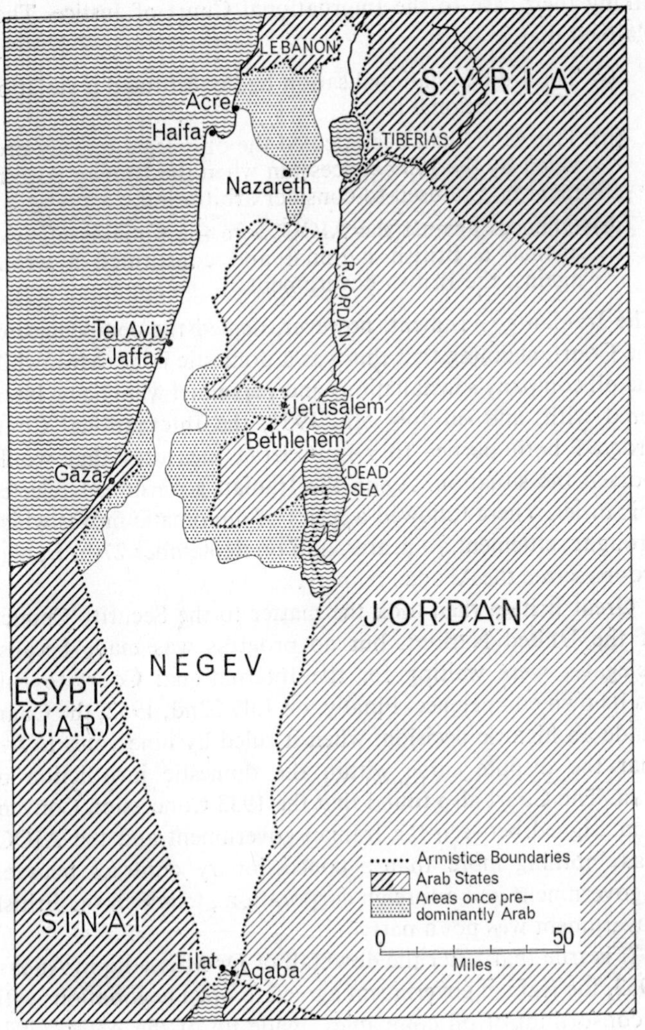

9 The State of Israel

taking their case to the International Court of Justice. They claimed that:

(i) The Iranian nationalisation had constituted a violation of international law.

(ii) The AIOC had been denied the only legal remedy provided by the 1933 concession when the Iranian government had refused to consider arbitration.

(iii) Offences against the AIOC were the same as offences against a British national and constituted a wrong against the British government.

The Iranian government, however, denied the competence of the Court, claiming that this was a domestic issue. Meanwhile the oil company's installations and personnel were being interfered with, and on July 5th, 1951, the International Court ordered both parties to refrain from measures that would worsen the situation. Again the Iranian government rejected this order. There followed a series of diplomatic moves which brought settlement no nearer, and on September 27th, Iranian troops seized the Abadan refinery.

Great Britain then took the matter to the Security Council of the United Nations, but no progress was made because delegates were waiting for the International Court to rule on its own competence. Finally, on July 22nd, 1952, the Court made an historic decision, when it ruled by nine votes to five that the dispute came within the domestic jurisdiction of Iran. The Court also found that the 1933 Concession Convention, signed between the Iranian government and the AIOC, was 'nothing more than a concessionary contract between a government and a foreign corporation', to which the British government was not a party.

It is true that, after the downfall of Dr Mussadiq in August 1953, the Iranian government agreed to open negotiations with a consortium of oil companies, made up of the AIOC (40% share), five United States companies (40% share), Shell (14%

share) and the Compagnie Française des Pétroles (6% share), and a year later a settlement was reached, not only on the future operation of the oil industry in Iran, but on AIOC's claims for compensation. This episode, however, aroused bitter feelings in Great Britain and gave rise to two points of considerable significance:

1 The failure of the Security Council or the International Court to uphold the company's rights exposed a dilemma which faced law-abiding states in the post-war world. Article 2 (4) of the United Nations Charter forbids the unilateral use of force by member nations to protect the lives and property of their nationals in foreign lands, but the Anglo-Iranian oil dispute proved that no effective alternative had, up to that time, been devised. The Labour government in Great Britain was anxious to do nothing that would weaken the authority of the United Nations, and thus opened itself to charges of weakness which a future Conservative government determined at all costs to avoid.

2 By making it clear that the United States government would not support Great Britain in the use of force, President Truman demonstrated that Anglo-American relations in the Middle East still continued to run a chequered course. British imperial connections were embarrassing to a power which had few important interests in the Middle East and which saw no threat to world peace in Arab nationalism.

The loss of Iranian oil would have resulted in the return of petrol rationing in Great Britain, had it not been for the discovery and exploitation of another source of supply in Kuwait. This small sheikdom on the Persian Gulf was indeed the main beneficiary of the dispute.

G *The Suez Canal crisis, 1956:*

The Anglo-Egyptian dispute over the revision of the 1936 treaty began in 1946, and it did not end until 1954. In July 1947, Egypt complained to the Security Council of the United Nations against the presence of British troops on Egyptian territory, but the first real climax came in October 1951, when the Egyptian government denounced the suggested Middle East Defence Organisation and called upon the new British Conservative government to evacuate both the Canal Zone and the Sudan. For the next three years, negotiations continued amid an atmosphere of violence, culminating in the attack upon European property in Cairo in January 1952.

On the night of July 22nd–23rd, 1952, a military *coup d'état* overthrew the Palace government of King Farouk and brought to power a new régime, led at first by General Neguib and later by Colonel Nasser. It was with this new government that an agreement was reached in February 1953, offering self-determination to the Sudan within three years. Only the control of the Canal Zone remained to be settled, but pressure from back-bench Conservative MP's made it difficult for the British government to accept any withdrawal. Finally, however, in October 1954, Mr Anthony Eden met the Egyptian terms and the last British troops prepared to leave Egyptian territory.

It seems likely that Mr Eden gave way on this issue not only because he had come to believe that the base was no longer vital to the defence of the Middle East in the nuclear age, but also because he had learned to have some respect for Colonel Nasser and the new Egyptian government. It may be assumed that some of the bitterness which Mr Eden later exhibited towards Colonel Nasser was due to a feeling of personal betrayal, accentuated by the sniping criticisms of many of his own party who had never forgiven him for the 'scuttle' of 1954.

1 The Suez Canal crisis did not begin with the Act of Nationalisation on July 26th, 1956. For more than a year it had been obvious that Russia was taking a far greater interest in Middle Eastern affairs. For example:

(i) On April 15th, 1955, the Russian government condemned the Baghdad Pact (*see page 126*) and gave warning of an active Russian response.

(ii) On July 21st, 1955, Mr Shepilov arrived in Cairo, an event which gave rise to a number of agreements and rumours.

(iii) In September 1955, Colonel Nasser announced the completion of an 'arms deal' with the Russian government.

(iv) During the spring of 1956 (at the time of the Russian 'peace offensive') Mr Sobolev, the Russian delegate to the United Nations, made certain positive (if decidedly pro-Arab) suggestions for preserving the Arab-Israeli peace settlement.

(v) In June 1956, a joint statement was issued from Damascus expressing the desire of Syria and Russia for increased co-operation, and a similar communiqué was issued from Beirut a week or so later.

Moreover, in July 1956, Colonel Nasser met Mr Nehru and President Tito at Brioni in Yugoslavia. At the end of their conference they issued a joint communiqué which emphasised their belief in the Ten Principles of the Bandung Conference, 1955 (*see page 89*), and clearly indicated that Egypt was now determined to follow a 'neutralist' foreign policy. To the West, this seemed bad enough, but many statesmen felt convinced that the Russo-Egyptian arms-deal and the other trade treaties which preceded it would inevitably reduce Colonel Nasser to the position of a puppet of Russia, and also provide for the extension of communism into the Middle East.

It was because of this that Mr Foster Dulles, the American

Secretary of State, abruptly withdrew the United States' offer of financial aid for the Aswan Dam. Mr Dulles's biographer writes of the affront, 'It had to be forthright, carrying its own built-in moral for neutrals . . .' It was now believed that, because the Aswan Dam was so important to the Egyptian economy, Colonel Nasser would be faced with only three possibilities:

(i) He could resign.
(ii) He could ask for a loan from Russia and thus confirm the West's charge that he was pro-communist.
(iii) He could become reconciled to the West on its terms.

In the event, he chose, on July 26th, 1956, to nationalise the Suez Canal Company, in such a way that the West could not claim an act of appropriation. Article 1 of the Canal Company Nationalisation Law stated 'Shareholders and holders of constituent shares shall be compensated in accordance with the value of the shares on the Paris stockmarket on the day preceding the enforcement of this law.'

2 The British, French and United States governments were not slow to react to this unexpected event. Mr Dulles complained that 'Egypt's seizure of the Suez Canal strikes a grievous blow at international confidence.' At Westminster, Mr Selwyn Lloyd (then Foreign Secretary) said, 'We feel that this great international waterway is not to be left at the mercy, caprice or spleen or hatred of one power or one man', and the French Prime Minister, M. Guy Mollet, spoke of taking 'energetic action' in response to Nasser's move.

Before the end of July, Great Britain had frozen Egypt's sterling balances and France had imposed her own economic sanctions. In early August, the British government called up certain army reservists, but the most publicised line of policy was directed towards the calling of a 24-nation conference, to which both Russia and Egypt were invited.

Though Colonel Nasser refused to attend, eighteen nations met at the first London Conference on August 16th, and, after rejecting a suggested compromise from Mr Krishna Menon, gave its support—though not unanimously—to Mr Dulles's suggestion for internationalisation of the canal. A further proposal to send Mr Menzies to Cairo to discuss it with Colonel Nasser was also carried.

Meanwhile, a considerable military build-up in the Mediterranean had so alarmed the British Labour Party that they demanded an assurance that the government was not preparing to invade Egypt. The Menzies mission was a failure, and led to another attempt by the Western nations to overcome Colonel Nasser's obstinacy. The Suez Canal Users Association was formed as a rival body to the Egyptian government, which had already begun to collect tolls from passing ships; and the canal pilots were encouraged to leave their posts and seek new employment with this organisation. It was hoped that without trained pilots, the Egyptian government would be unable to maintain the free passage of ships and that most of those nations who used the canal would, in future, pay their dues to the S.C.U.A. This strategy, however, did not work. Other pilots arrived from Russia and elsewhere, and United States' ships were instructed to pay their dues to Egypt.

Meanwhile, discussions were going on in the Security Council, and unofficially in the lobbies of the United Nations, but any hopes of a settlement were ruined by the Israeli invasion of Egypt on October 29th, and the Anglo-French decision to present an ultimatum to the Israeli and Egyptian governments. This ultimatum, which was issued on October 30th, the same day that Great Britain and France vetoed two resolutions in the Security Council urging all members of the United Nations to refrain from the use of threat or force in the Middle East, demanded that both the belligerents should withdraw their forces to lines ten miles to the east and west of Suez. The Israeli government saw fit to accept this demand, but Colonel Nasser rejected it unceremoniously.

On October 31st, the Anglo-French invasion of the Port Said area began.

3 The significance of these events in the Middle East was heightened by the rising in Budapest (*see pages 59–67*), which began on October 23rd and resulted in Russian intervention to defeat the attempts of the Hungarian nationalists to rid themselves of a detested communist régime. The Russian government used its veto in the Security Council to prevent discussion of the Hungarian situation, and it was not until November 8th, when Russian armoured forces had almost regained control of Budapest, that the General Assembly finally got down to discussing it. On November 9th a motion was passed calling upon Russia to withdraw its forces from Hungary, and on November 21st, another condemned Russia for failing to do so.

In fact, the initiative of the General Assembly had been more effective in the Middle East. On November 3rd the British and French governments agreed to accept a United Nations' resolution of the previous day, calling for a cease-fire, provided that an effective United Nations' force was formed and accepted by both Israel and Egypt. The first suggestion of a United Nations' force had been made by Mr Lester Pearson, and on November 4th this idea was accepted by the General Assembly.

The cease-fire took effect from midnight on November 6th, and the United Nations Emergency Force began to arrive on November 15th. How far the Anglo-French decision to accept the cease-fire was affected by the resolutions of the United Nations, and whether they were influenced by the Bulganin note of November 5th, which threatened to use force to halt their aggression, we do not know.

H *The consequences of the Suez affair:*

As a result of their intervention at Suez, any remaining Anglo-French influence in the Middle East was, for some time to come, replaced by feelings of hostility and suspicion. Despite her repressive measures in Hungary, the resolutions against which were strangely dismissed as 'an imperialist plot', Russia gained immense prestige in the Middle East, and in 1958 she offered to finance the Aswan Dam project.

Anglo-American relations were, of course, greatly strained by the whole affair, for not only had the United States voted with Russia against Great Britain in the Security Council, but it was felt in Great Britain that Mr Dulles, who had precipitated events by withdrawing U.S. aid for the Aswan Dam, should have stood fast with his allies as the results of his action began to unfold. Moreover, there were British MP's who fostered a latent anti-Americanism in Great Britain by maintaining that the real motives behind the refusal of the United States to discipline Colonel Nasser lay in their desire to replace Great Britain as the new power in the Middle East. The Russians certainly feared that this might come about, and when the United States government accepted the Israeli claim to freedom of shipping in the Gulf of Aqaba, they made the most of its propaganda value. Similarly, when President Eisenhower spoke to Congress on January 5th, 1957, about a military vacuum in the Middle East, and promised help for any state which felt itself threatened by communism, he presented the Russian government with another opportunity to weaken United States' influence in the area.

Mr Khrushchev had been quick to realise how tender are the emotions of newly independent states, and when he heard

President Eisenhower drawing attention to their military weakness, he knew that the Eisenhower Doctrine would have very limited effect in the Middle East. Certainly, despite the visit of King Saud to the United States and the pro-Western attitude of King Hussein of Jordan, a communiqué issued after a four-power Arab Summit Conference emphasised not only the 'policy of impartiality and positive neutrality' which all Arab states would follow, but also 'the fact that the defence of the Arab world should emanate from the Arab world itself in the light of its own security and outside the sphere of foreign pacts'.

I *Crises arising out of the United States' search for a new defence policy in the Middle East:*

In 1957 and 1958 the United States attempted to restore Western defences in the Middle East. She played a more active part in the affairs of the Baghdad Pact, but her efforts to strengthen the southern tier of defence by persuading Arab states to accept the Eisenhower Doctrine led to a confused period of intrigue and revolution.

1 In early 1957 the most Western of all Arab states, the Lebanon, accepted United States' aid and announced its adherence to the Doctrine; other Arab states, however, did not fail to notice that this coincided with the visit of the U.S.S. *Forrestal* to Beirut and a considerable display of United States' air power from the carrier.

2 King Hussein of Jordan also announced his acceptance of United States' protection, but not before he had first overthrown Prime Minister Nabulsi and then the Khalidi Cabinet. It is very difficult to discover whether these dismissals caused, or were the result of, internal troubles, but there can be no doubt that a dangerous situation arose in Jordan in

April 1957. Had not the U.S. Sixth Fleet sailed swiftly to the eastern Mediterranean, there might have been a rising in Amman, supported by both Egypt and Syria.

3 On August 21st, 1957, President Eisenhower declared at a news conference that Syria had fallen under communist influence, and the British *Daily Express* reported that thousands of Russian volunteers were arriving there by sea and air. Mr Loy Henderson was sent as a United States' envoy to Istanbul, but was refused permission to enter Syria, whose government now proclaimed that Turkish troops were massed upon her frontier, ready to invade. On September 10th, Mr Gromyko supported this, and the next day, Bulganin officially warned the Turkish government. It seemed that another full-scale crisis was about to erupt into war, but neither side was anxious to precipitate this, and tension eased when a resolution was accepted in the General Assembly of the United Nations, calling upon the states of the Middle East to live together in friendship and to seek conciliation.

4 In early 1958, two events of considerable importance occurred. On February 1st came the announcement of union between Syria and Egypt, who were to be joined later by the Yemen. This new United Arab Republic obviously became a new force in Middle Eastern affairs, but it is believed by some that its inception came about as a result of Syrian initiative rather than Egyptian imperialism. It did, however, affect United States' policy in the Middle East, for Washington was still not prepared to accept neutralism in the 'cold war', and there was no chance that the new U.A.R. would accept the Eisenhower Doctrine. It is not therefore surprising that on February 14th, the pro-Western King Feisal of Iraq and his cousin, King Hussein of Jordan, announced the formation of the Arab Federation.

It seemed that a balance of forces had been achieved in the Middle East which might now permit a period of stability, but this was not to be.

5 In the Lebanon, a revolution developed when President Chamoun, who had accepted the Eisenhower Doctrine, attempted to perpetuate himself in office, against the rule of the constitution. Western statesmen accused the U.A.R. of infiltration into the Lebanon from Syria, and a new build-up began in the eastern Mediterranean. The United States Sixth Fleet returned to the area and British troops were hastily flown to Cyprus. Meanwhile, the Prime Minister of Iraq, Nuri es Said, flew to London for consultations, and a meeting of the Moslem countries of the Baghdad Pact was arranged, to be held in Ankara on July 14th, 1958.

Again, we are uncertain of the facts in this affair. The West claimed that Russian-inspired aggression against the Lebanon and Jordan was being planned from the U.A.R., but many neutral sources rejected this suggestion and preferred to look upon the whole incident as another Western attempt to find excuses for military intervention: this time, Prime Minister Nuri es Said, King Hussein and President Chamoun would fight alongside their allies to occupy Syria, and then turn southwards against Egypt.

We may never know the truth, for, on the night of July 14th, General Kassim initiated a revolution in Baghdad, murdered King Feisal, Crown Prince Ilahi and Nuri es Said and prevented any possible Iraqi action against her neighbours. The next day United States' marines landed in the Lebanon, and on July 17th British troops began to land in Jordan. It may be that, once again, their presence stabilised a dangerous situation, for the monarchy in Jordan was most insecure, and the rising in Beirut had developed into a full-scale civil war.

J *The Middle East in the 1960's:*

Though the situation in the Middle East is likely to remain fluid for some time to come, the early 1960's have provided certain significant pointers towards the future:

1 The withdrawal of Syria from the United Arab Republic in September 1961, seemed to be a setback for President Nasser and his supporters, but events in February and March, 1963, indicated that a new and more acceptable Arab union or federation was going to emerge. In February, a coalition of Iraqi army officers and men who shared the Egyptian President's hopes of 'Arab unity' and 'Arab socialism', engineered a *coup d'état* in Baghdad, in which General Kassim was murdered and his government destroyed. The new Iraqi government, under Colonel Aref, immediately expressed a wish to co-operate with Egypt, and was supported in this policy by a new Syrian government, which took office in March after a successful military plot in Damascus.

2 It has indeed been suggested that the adherence of Jordan to the new United Arab Republic could only promote stability in the Middle East, for a strong Arab Federation would not fear attack and might be brought to offer diplomatic recognition of Israel. From the Israeli point of view, such a move might at first be viewed with horror, and talk of preventive war has already been heard, but ultimately, they too may come to recognise that a politically contented Arab people are likely to be more interested in economic development than in arousing the anger of the Western world—particularly the U.S.A.—by any incursion into Israeli territory. Arab-Israeli hostility, however, though subdued, continued to exist during the 1960's, and in October 1965 there occurred a number of clashes between Israel and Jordan which gave little hope of any speedy improvement in the relationships between Arab and Jew.

3 Meanwhile, in the Yemen, the revolt which began in September 1962, when a group of officers and politicians in San'a forced the Imam to seek refuge with the loyal tribes of the north, developed into a full-scale civil war. This assumed a more menacing aspect when the kings of Jordan and Saudi Arabia supported the loyal Yemeni forces with arms and money, and President Nasser began supplying troops and equipment to Marshal Sallal and the new republican régime.

In 1963, a United Nations' 'disengagement plan' provided that the Saudi Arabians should stop all aid to the royalists, whilst the Egyptians undertook to withdraw their troops from the Yemen; but this quickly broke down, and instead of peace coming to the area, fighting spread to the South Arabia Federation. There, in the mountainous Radfan areas, rebellious tribesmen, furnished with arms from the Yemeni Republic, began to threaten the legitimate rulers—the sheiks who had entered into alliance with Great Britain. This revolt threatened the security of the British base at Aden and forced the British government to order a series of land and air strikes in defence of their royal allies in the South Arabia Federation. This newly created federal state was seen in Great Britain as a means of protecting Aden from hostile outside interference, and Aden itself was regarded by the British government and opposition in 1964 as a most necessary base for the protection of British oil interests throughout the Middle East.

It is possible that a reappraisal of Great Britain's defence needs east of Suez may reverse this policy during the years to come; but this will not happen quickly, though the agreement made between President Nasser and King Feisal in August 1965 to end the fighting in the Yemen may have assisted the process.

20 Africa

It is likely that the 1960's will be the decisive decade in the evolution of Africa, though its political and economic future defies the imagination at the moment of writing.

AFRICAN NATIONALISM

Despite the many divergencies and inconsistencies to be found in this vast continent, it is possible to discern some pattern in the events now taking place. Nationalism in Africa is almost indefinable: it cuts across tribal customs, races and religions; it accepts artificial political boundaries which were first imposed upon the African scene by the European powers at the end of the nineteenth century; it has no single prophet—no Joan of Arc, no Gandhi; but everywhere its major task is the same, to oppose colonialism until independence has been achieved. In this great movement, the Berber sees himself as the brother of the Swazi, and the Zulu works alongside the Arab. Pan-Africanism has already made its appearance, but its leadership and its future development have yet to be decided.

All the European powers have now come to recognise the 'wind of change' which is blowing through Africa, and they all envisage some kind of partnership. Difficulties have arisen, however, because originally only Great Britain planned for the day when there should be a general democratic emergence of the Africans, and for some, her plans were suspect. Until recently, France and Belgium offered partnership only to those Africans who could reach the required social and economic standards, and made no attempt to train the masses for the day when they would have to govern themselves. Despite this lack of political education, however, French West Africa, Morocco, Tunisia and, at last, Algeria, are accepting the challenge of independence which they have won, in most cases after years of terrorism and civil war. Now, having been accepted as associate members of the Common Market, they may well find their economic path smoother than they anticipated, though they will be careful to avoid any further subordination to a European bloc, be it economic or political.

When Belgium suddenly offered independence to the Congo in 1960, the full significance of her earlier policies soon made itself felt. The Congolese were expected to rule themselves, in a land three times as big as western Europe, with its economic resources concentrated in one area, its people ranging from the primitive pygmy and the seven-foot giant of the Watutsi tribe to the few sophisticated urban dwellers of Leopoldville or Elisabethville. Moreover, there existed a well of hatred for Europeans, who symbolised all that the ruling power had stood for over the past sixty or seventy years. Little wonder that, when the Belgian government withdrew from the Congo, an explosive situation arose which might well have provided the point of entry for communism into Africa, and which certainly did present the United Nations Organisation with its greatest challenge until that date. One cannot help wondering whether similar situations might one day arise in Portuguese Angola or Mozambique, where, at the moment, the European power remains master of the situation, but political liberties for the Africans scarcely exist.

A similar fear of native revolution is present in the Republic of South Africa where, since the Afrikaners were granted independence by Great Britain in 1910, they have worked successfully to overthrow the liberalising tendencies of the Cape British and have now adopted a policy of *apartheid* (racial segregation), the implications of which might well have overflowed into the British territories of Central Africa. There, the ideal of permanent white supremacy coming from the south clashed with the impatient and often arrogant nationalist influences which swept down from the north and west. In this

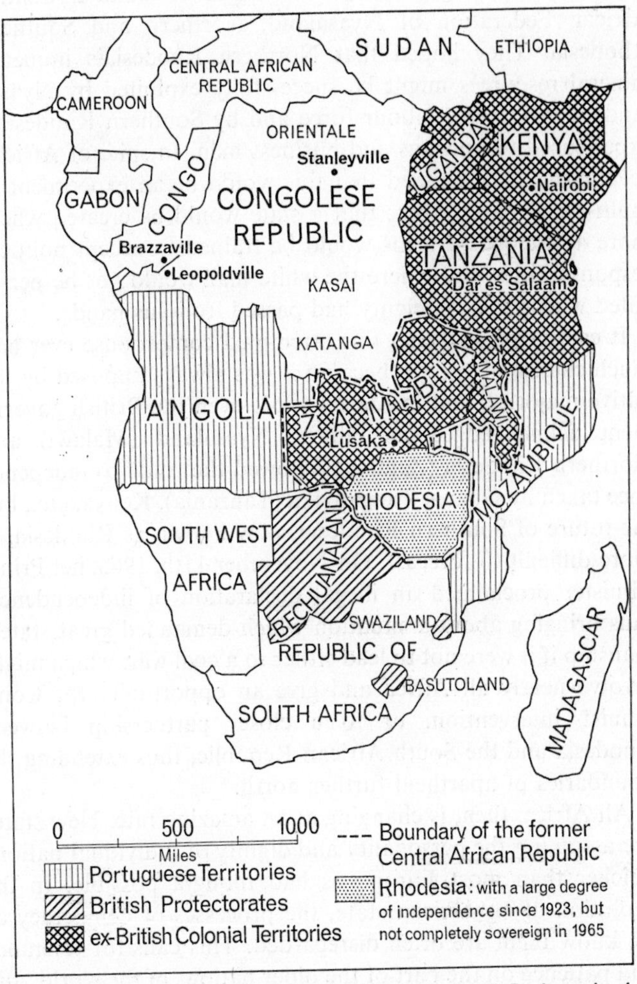

10 Southern Africa. Both Basutoland (Lesotho) and Bechuanaland (Botswana) attain independence in 1966.

area, the British government attempted to build a Central African Federation of Nyasaland, Northern and Southern Rhodesia. They hoped that Northern Rhodesia's immense mineral resources might be successfully exploited by Nyasaland's considerable labour force and by Southern Rhodesia's experienced technicians and business men. In spite of African scepticism, they claimed that this would be an experiment in multi-racial partnership; that a state would be created where more and more Africans would be trained to accept political responsibilities, but where the white man would not be persecuted when the sovereignty had passed from his hands.

It cannot be said that this attempted compromise ever had much chance of success because it was always opposed by the native majority, and in March 1963, even the British government acknowledged its failure. Nyasaland (Malawi) and Northern Rhodesia (Zambia) followed the route to independence taken by Ghana, Tanganyika (Tanzania), Kenya, etc., but the future of Southern Rhodesia, now known as Rhodesia, is more difficult to forecast. On November 11th, 1965, her Prime Minister proclaimed an illegal declaration of independence, thus bringing about a situation which demanded great statesmanship if it were not to lead either to a civil war, which might involve nearly all Africa and give an opportunity for Communist intervention, or to a closer partnership between Rhodesia and the South African Republic, thus extending the boundaries of apartheid further north.

All Africa, then, is changing at an amazing rate. New states are assuming the personality and dignity of individual nations quicker than most Europeans had thought possible. In the evolution of an African state, the processes of democracy as we know them are often disregarded. This calls for tolerance and patience on the part of the older nations of the world, and for economic assistance and planning on an international level. (*See Chapter 26, page 213.*)

ALGERIA

A *French colonial policy in Algeria:*

France began her conquest of Algeria in 1830, and quickly initiated a policy of colonisation by offering confiscated land, not only to soldiers and their families, but to wealthy French companies who soon acquired large holdings. As far as administration was concerned, the Algerian settlers soon began to show their hostility to any central direction from Paris. Before the close of the nineteenth century, they had begun to demand equality with metropolitan France, but it was not until 1947 that an act was passed which established a separate administration for Algeria and promised financial autonomy and French citizenship for all Algerians. This statute, however, made it very clear that the Arab population of Algeria was to remain largely disenfranchised. The new constitution saw to it that political power was retained by the settlers, who rigged the elections and continued to legislate in their own interests, with little regard for the seemingly insignificant nationalist groups who formed the very weak opposition within the Algerian Assembly. Yet it was in that same year, 1947, that an organisation was formed to plan a revolution for the early 1950's. Arab nationalism was astir, and even when the French discovered the plot and arrested some of the leaders, those who escaped fled to Cairo to organise further resistance. Led by Ben Bella, Ferhat Abbas and Mohamed Khider, they formed the Front de la Libération Nationale (F.L.N.), and in November 1954, they ordered rebellion to begin throughout Algeria.

B *The Civil War:*

The history of the civil war that followed was complicated by the internal divisions on both sides. The French settlers were supported by those in France who demanded an 'Algérie

Française', but were opposed by all French liberals; whilst among the Arab nationalists, hatred grew up between the moderates, who wanted co-operation with France, and the extremists, whose acts of terrorism and torture provoked an equally inhuman response from the French army on the spot.

No government in Paris seemed able to cope with the situation. Guy Mollet tried to introduce a programme of 'Pacification, Reforms and Elections', but when he visited Algiers in February 1956, he was met with such hostility that he was forced to give up the conciliatory plan, and instead, granted more power to the settlers, who were now well organised by Pierre Lagaillarde. There followed the capture of five F.L.N. leaders, including Ben Bella, as they were being flown to a conciliatory conference in Tunis, organised by President Bourguiba and Mohammed V, King of Morocco. Against orders, the French pilots of the royal aircraft flew from Morocco to Algiers, thus ending any chance of reasonable negotiations.

At last, in the spring of 1958, it seemed that the new Pflimlin government was about to try, once again, to come to terms with the nationalists. On May 13th a crowd in the centre of Algiers began to sack government offices and called upon the popular General Massu, Commander of the Tenth Parachute Division, to act as their leader. This he agreed to do, and set up a Committee of Public Safety for the temporary government of Algeria; at the same time he called for the return of General de Gaulle to power in Paris.

In the face of this military insurrection, for the army had joined the Europeans in Algeria, M. Pflimlin resigned, the Fourth Republic came to an end and, on June 1st, General de Gaulle took over the government of France.

The situation which developed in the following months was complicated in the extreme. At one time General de Gaulle spoke of 'pacifying Algeria so that it would always be body and soul of France', whilst on another occasion he referred to an

'Algerian personality' and made no mention of integration with France. By 1960, however, a further test of strength between the new government in Paris and the extremists in Algeria could no longer be delayed. General de Gaulle had, by then, proposed self-determination for Algeria, and his dismissal of General Massu, the hero of May 1958, caused another insurrection on January 24th, led by Joseph Ortiz and Pierre Lagaillarde. This time, however, the army remained loyal and the incipient rebellion collapsed. There followed a purge of army and civilian leaders; Jaques Soustelle was dismissed from his post as Minister Designate in Algiers, and in Paris General de Gaulle was given extraordinary powers to rule by decree. It was, indeed, becoming obvious that Algeria would be offered her independence in the end, and this led to a final attempt at revolt by Generals Challe, Zeller, Jouhaud and Salan on April 22nd, 1961. For a few hours the army hesitated, and during that time, some of the Parachutists and Foreign Legion occupied Algiers and proclaimed martial law in the name of the O.A.S. (Secret Army Organisation). The insurrection lasted for four days, but when it became known that the majority of the army had again remained loyal, General Challe surrendered and Algiers was re-occupied.

C *The Evian Agreement and after:*

On May 10th, 1961, the French government announced formal cease-fire negotiations, which would begin ten days later at Evian les Bains. Though these soon ran into difficulties, a settlement was finally signed on March 18th, 1962. This provided certain safeguards for Europeans who decided to remain in Algeria, in return for French economic and financial aid. Algeria would remain in the franc zone and would invite French investment. In return, France would buy Algerian wine and agricultural produce, and her oil companies working in the Sahara would retain their privileged position for six years.

France was also allowed to keep the naval base at Mers el Kebir for a further fifteen years, after which the agreement would have to be negotiated anew, but the Foreign Legion was to be evacuated to Corsica and other French armed forces were to remain in Algeria for three years only.

The Evian Agreement was a compromise which offered certain benefits to both sides, but it was unlikely that the Algerian government would consider it to be the final word. Mr Ben Bella soon referred to the need for revision in pursuit of 'social justice for all Algerians of all origins', and there can be little doubt that he hoped to obtain a larger share of the Sahara oil and mineral profits, which have greatly increased since the rich deposits were discovered in 1957. Independence did not bring an end to terrorism, for the O.A.S. appealed to all Europeans to fight on, and for a time in the spring and early summer of 1962, it seemed that the peace agreement, which had been approved by an overwhelming majority of Frenchmen in the referendum of April 8th, would be sabotaged. Thousands of settlers, however, continued to leave Algeria, and this, plus the determination of de Gaulle's government, persuaded the O.A.S. leaders to come to terms with the nationalists, which they did on June 17th, 1962, when a truce was signed.

This did not end the problems of the Algerian government. The French now released about a million Moslems who had been kept in detention camps during the war, and these, in addition to the return of thousands more from Morocco and Tunis, increased the danger of famine, which was only averted by the action of such bodies as the International Red Cross, OXFAM (the Oxford Committee for Famine Relief) and their counterparts in other lands. Moreover, a split quickly developed between the nationalists themselves, and fighting actually broke out again between the supporters of the various groups.

Out of this confused situation, the left-wing anti-colonialist

Ben Bella, who had been imprisoned for five and a half years and had thus played little part in the peace negotiations, triumphed over Ben Khedda, his more moderate opponent. When elections finally took place in September 1962, Ben Bella was elected Prime Minister by 141 votes out of the 189 cast. Although he pledged himself to build a socialist Arab state in Algeria and visited Dr Castro in Cuba, Ben Bella banned the Communist Party in his country and stated his intention to follow a neutralist foreign policy. Certainly, his programme of agrarian reform and industrialisation 'to absorb our unemployed masses' proved to be impossible without outside help, and soon Europeans with technical and educational qualifications were encouraged to return, whilst French financial aid for 1963 was to be over a thousand million francs. Undoubtedly, Ben Bella hoped to win further aid from both East and West and from the various agencies of the United Nations, and when he was overthrown by the Algerian Army, led by Colonel Boumedienne, on June 19th, 1965, he had already established very close relations with the U.S.S.R. and was held in great esteem by all Afro-Asian Heads of State.

Colonel Boumedienne, though Moslem where Ben Bella was secularist, is nonetheless a convinced Socialist, and has consequently brought about no significant change in government policy. For example, the negotiations for the revision of the Evian Agreement, started by Ben Bella, were brought to a successful conclusion in July 1965 when a new Franco-Algerian Co-operative Agreement was signed. This allowed for the joint exploitation of petroleum and natural gas in the most promising areas, and for French economic aid and investment in the industrial development of the country.

After the terrorism of the 1950's, it now seems possible that a new and prosperous relationship is about to develop between France and an independent Algeria, with multi-lateral investment and trade kept under the strictest control.

THE CONGO

A *The Belgian Congo and the granting of independence, 1960:* From 1908, when the administration of the Congo Free State was handed over to the Belgian government, until 1960, when it was almost rushed into independence, this vast area of Africa was held by some to be a model of effective repression and by others to be an example of paternalism at its best. The 'Belgian method', as it was called, dismissed any idea of African democracy as romantic nonsense; on the other hand, it encouraged the Congolese people to develop their skills and to share in the great wealth of the country. A rigid discipline was imposed from above, but provided that politics were left to the Belgian administrators, the natives in the Congo could look forward to a standard of living higher than anywhere in foreign-dominated Africa.

Two factors made revolution in the Congo inevitable, however. In furtherance of their system, the Belgian government had encouraged the development of an African middle class which, they believed, would be conservative and stable; but it was just these newly educated and 'evolved' African lawyers, doctors and traders who proved to be dissatisfied with their politically inferior status. Poverty-stricken natives do not initiate rebellion, but throughout Africa, as throughout Europe in the nineteenth century, the great nationalist movements have begun when education has stimulated thought. In the Congo, it is true that in 1960 the new African middle class was still very small, but it did exist, and grew more and more discontented as it assimilated the news of political progress made in other African territories. This, indeed, was the second, all-important factor which could not be denied. The Belgians could not hope to separate the Congo from its neighbours, however much they might try to control communication with the outside world.

That the *status quo* in the Congo did not persist for another decade or so is due to a combination of events that occurred from 1957 onwards. In that year, copper prices suddenly fell, and unemployment deepened anti-Belgian feeling; at the same time, Congolese nationalists were taking very seriously the writings of Mr A. A. J. von Bilsen, who proclaimed the end of nineteenth-century imperialism, a forecast which was given added weight by the decision of General de Gaulle in August 1958 to offer independence to those Congolese territories administered by France.

Meanwhile, preparations were being made for the all-African Peoples' Congress, to be held in Accra at the end of that same year. Representing the Congolese people at that Congress was M. Patrice Lumumba, a great follower of Dr Nkrumah and leader of the new Mouvement National Congolais. His return to the Congo coincided with riots of the unemployed in Leopoldville, and with the arrest and exile of another great nationalist, Mr Joseph Kasavubu.

It seemed that further persecution would follow, and that the road to Congolese independence would have to take the usual bloody path, when suddenly—almost overnight—the Belgian government, acting on the advice of a Parliamentary Commission investigating the troubles in Leopoldville, sought to protect its economic assets in the Congo by offering independence almost at once.

B *Independence and its consequences:*

From its first announcement, this policy was regarded with some scepticism by colonial administrators in Europe and by moderates in Africa, for the Belgians were leaving the Congo with no experienced politicians, no planned constitution, no civil servants and, above all, no time in which to provide these vital necessities of state. The events that followed were thus foreseen by many observers, but the whole situation was made even worse by the internal divisions which began to appear in the Congo, and by communist attempts to enter African affairs through the chaos and anarchy which ensued.

Briefly, the domestic difficulties centred around the quarrels which developed amongst the Congolese nationalists. The followers of Kasavubu wanted to establish a loose federation of autonomous areas in the Congo which would go some way to preserve the various tribal groups to which many Congolese still remained loyal. Lumumba and his supporters, on the other hand, considered this plan to be reactionary and inefficient: for them, the only answer could be a strong unitary state with a powerful central government. From the beginning, this conflict inflamed passions and threatened to destroy the viability of the country, because alongside Mr Kasavubu stood Mr Tshombe, leader of the Katanga, without whose mineral wealth the remainder of the Congo would soon plunge into bankruptcy.

Eventually, some sort of compromise was hastily worked out, and Mr Kasavubu became President of the new republic, with Mr Lumumba as his first Prime Minister. It is doubtful whether these two men could have worked together for long in the best of circumstances, but the granting of independence to the Congo was immediately followed by a complete breakdown of law and order.

The Congolese people, suddenly released from years of humiliation and servitude, began to commit the most heinous crimes not only against the hated Europeans in their midst, but against each other. Chaos ensued, and in spite of Mr Lumumba's protests, the Belgian government found it necessary to send some five thousand paratroops back into the Congo to protect the persons and property of its nationals. Even Mr Lumumba realised that outside help was necessary, but he hoped to find it in the Security Council of the United Nations which, by agreeing to send a military police force to the Congo, embarked upon a course of action unprecedented in the history of that organisation.

C *United Nations action in the Congo—the secession of Katanga:*

Despite all the mistakes which were made by U.N. Commanders on the spot, and accepting the fact that the U.N. tended to drift from one crisis to another with no clear policy in view, it is certain that the United Nations' intervention not only saved the Congo from disintegration, but, by its presence, helped to bring about the withdrawal of communist influence from the new republic.

The split between Kasavubu and Lumumba, together with the existence of a third régime led by Colonel Mobutu, meant that there were now three mutually hostile Congolese governments. An even more serious situation, however, arose in July 1960, when Mr Tshombe declared that Katanga would remain independent. This development represented the most difficult problem facing the United Nations in their task of re-unification.

In this struggle, the United Nations faced not only Mr Tshombe's Katangese troops, but some 3,500 Belgians and mercenaries in addition to the wealth and world-wide influence of the Union Minière. In August 1961, the Security Council passed a resolution ordering the U.N. troops to seize these mercenaries, in furtherance of their earlier mandate 'to prevent the occurrence of civil war in the Congo, including the use of force if necessary in the last resort'. This led directly to an outbreak of war in Katanga between the U.N. and Mr Tshombe's forces, which continued from September 1st to September 20th, when a cease-fire was arranged.

Before the start of the Katanga action, the diamond state of South Kasai had accepted the authority of President Kasavubu's central government under the new Prime Minister,

Mr Adoula. At the same time, following the assassination of Mr Lumumba, the Stanleyville régime had agreed to merge with the central government. Looking back on these developments, Dr Conor Cruise O'Brien, the U.N. Commander on the spot, has since maintained that it would have been possible to convince Mr Tshombe of U.N. determination in August, and that it was the great copper interests of Katanga that were in fact responsible for the bloodshed in September. This suggestion was hotly debated in the councils of the world, for the West as well as the East was often critical of the United Nations' role in the Congo. If Mr Khrushchev talked of the U.N. forces bolstering up colonialism, right-wing sympathisers in Western capitals have condemned the U.N. for participation in a civil war.

Nevertheless, a peaceful settlement seemed to be in sight when Mr Hammarskjoeld, Secretary-General of the United Nations Organisation, decided to meet Mr Tshombe at Ndola in Northern Rhodesia. The Secretary-General, however, was killed when his plane crashed during that flight, and the fighting continued. Finally, increased United States' pressure persuaded Mr Tshombe to meet Mr Adoula, the Prime Minister of the central government, and some basis for negotiation was agreed upon.

Months went by, however, and the Congo remained disunited and unsettled. Discussions were held in Leopoldville about the integration of Katangese forces in the national army, about the division of the mining revenue and the establishment of a common currency, but little progress was made and Mr Tshombe began to hint at a possible future union of the Katanga with the Central African Federation.

In August 1962, U Thant, the new Secretary-General of the United Nations, put forward his own plan for the re-unification of the Congo, and suggested that, if Mr Tshombe refused to accept it, Katanga should be forced to end secession by a trade embargo or further use of U.N. force if necessary. Mr Tshombe quickly announced his acceptance of the plan, though he attempted to protract negotiations even at this late stage.

In October 1962, a proposed federal constitution for the Congo was published, which created twenty-one provinces, but which divided Katanga into two and took away most of her real power. Whilst Mr Tshombe's government were debating the new proposals, a breakdown of discipline amongst Katangese forces gave the U.N. an opportunity to resume operations, and, in January 1963, they launched a successful offensive against the main strongholds of Mr Tshombe's forces. At last, the end of secession had been achieved, but it remained to be seen whether the central government at Leopoldville would be able to pay its debts and rid the country of the bad feelings which had been engendered almost everywhere since 1960. It was certain that Mr Adoula would have to rely upon United States' and United Nations' aid, and should he fail to get it, it seemed probable that his régime might be forced to give way to one that would look to Moscow or Peking for assistance.

D *Developments in the Congo 1964–65:*

During 1964 so many rebellions broke out in various provinces of the Congo that President Kasavubu was forced to dismiss the ineffective Mr Adoula and recall Mr Tshombe from exile in Europe. From being Premier of a possible secessionist Katanga, Mr Tshombe now found himself Prime Minister of the Congo Federation. Moreover, in June 1964 the United Nations Force, which had been preserving some sort of order in the Congo, was withdrawn, and Mr Tshombe, determined to put down the rebels, replaced it with white mercenaries recruited from South Africa and Europe.

This had the effect of increasing rebel activity and, aided by the Chinese Communists, the rebels advanced from Burundi along the shores of Lake Tanganyika. Soon they were in control of most of the eastern provinces, including the town of Stanleyville where some thousand white hostages were taken. To protect these men, women and children, Belgian paratroopers were flown into the area by the United States Air Force from the British base on Ascension Island. On November 24th they took Stanleyville, freed most of the white hostages and set about the more difficult task of searching for other Europeans who had disappeared from outlying districts. Eventually this was completed and the paratroopers were withdrawn, leaving Mr Tshombe, his mercenaries and the Congolese National Army to pacify the country.

During 1965 they achieved some success, but it was a slow business. The rebels continued to receive Chinese aid through Brazzaville and were known to have the sympathy of President Nasser and Dr Nkrumah. Then, in October 1965, Mr Tshombe was himself replaced by Mr Kimba as Prime Minister, and the scene seemed set for a political battle between President Kasavubu and Mr Tshombe in the Presidential elections due in 1966. Such was the intensity of feeling whipped up by this struggle for power, however, that General Joseph Mobutu, Commander of the Congo Army, saw fit to proclaim a five-year military régime, with himself as President, as the only way of forestalling a renewal of civil war in the Congo. Whether this bloodless *coup* will have the desired effect, time alone will tell.

SOUTH AFRICA

A *The struggle between the British and the Boers:*

In 1899, a century of growing hostility between the Afrikaners (Dutch colonisers who followed Jan van Reibeck and the Dutch East India Company to South Africa in 1653) and the British (who did not arrive in the Cape until the Napoleonic

Wars) came to a climax in the Boer War. This lasted for three years and was eventually won by the British, who were never quite sure about the justice of their cause, and in 1910 attempted to bring about a peaceful settlement by uniting the northern republics of the Transvaal and the Orange Free State with the British colonies of Natal and the Cape in a new self-governing Union of South Africa.

The Liberal government in Great Britain hoped that within this new state, the liberalising influences of the Cape and Natal, which had been opposed by the Boers since the days when slavery was abolished in the British Empire, would now have a chance to penetrate peacefully into the Transvaal and the Orange Free State. No attempt was made to protect the Africans in the Union, because, as yet, they scarcely warranted the attention even of Liberal England, which was, at that time, more interested in clearing its conscience of war-crimes supposedly committed against its Boer enemies.

It soon became clear, however, that the struggle between British and Boer had not yet been decided. Not only were liberal ideas rejected in the north, but, from the year 1924, when General Hertzog became the first Nationalist Prime Minister, the overthrow of liberalism in the Cape became merely a matter of time. It is true that, owing to the influence of General Smuts and his United Party, this process was somewhat delayed when the Union decided to join the Allies in the Second World War, but this was not a particularly popular decision, and in the early post-war era the Nationalist Party overwhelmed its political opponents and set itself firmly in office under its new leader, Dr Malan.

B *Apartheid:*

The road towards *apartheid* (racial segregation) was now open, for Afrikaners outnumbered Cape British by three to one, the

African had been removed from the common roll as early as 1936, and successive Nationalist governments consolidated the supremacy of the white man in South African society. The statute books from 1948 until the present day are full of Acts which aim at complete segregation of whites from Africans and 'Coloureds'. The Group Areas Act of 1950 set up racial areas in all large towns; the Natives Resettlement Act of 1954 removed some 75,000 Africans from the centre of Johannesburg. In 1955, the government passed the Bantu Education Act, which put the future education of Africans directly under the control of the state and permitted the Prime Minister, Dr Verwoerd, to say with certainty that 'there is no place for the native in European society above certain forms of labour'. In 1957, the Natives Law Amendment Act forbade all blacks and whites to meet together socially.

When the pent-up feelings of hatred caused by these measures led the Africans to riot in Durban in January 1960, the situation in South Africa became explosive. What seemed to be nothing but a peaceful demonstration in Sharpeville on March 21st, 1960, caused some of the police to open fire on an unarmed crowd. More than seventy Negroes were killed; but whilst this incident served to condemn the policy of apartheid in most of the capitals of the world, in South Africa it strengthened the hand of the Verwoerd government, which proclaimed a state of emergency under which action was taken to outlaw the Pan Africanist Conference and the more moderate African National Congress.

Further steps were also taken to complete the policy of segregation as soon as possible, so that, by 1963, plans were completed for the first 'Bantustan' in the Transkei. It was planned that this native state of 3½ million Xhosa people should have its own legislative assembly and should, in theory, develop economically, politically and socially in isolation from the remainder of the European south. Other tribal units were also envisaged as part of the apartheid policy, but two fundamental questions remain, as yet, unanswered. Will these Bantustans ever be able to provide an economic livelihood for their people, and, if so, will they be content to remain politically and socially inferior to the Europeans who surround them?

C *Withdrawal from the Commonwealth:*

Meanwhile, in March 1961, at the Conference of Commonwealth Prime Ministers, it was impossible to agree upon the re-admission of South Africa into the Commonwealth as a republic. On March 16th Dr Verwoerd's government, realising that other African and Asian members of the Commonwealth would never associate with South Africa so long as she maintained her policy of segregation, decided to leave the Commonwealth. The trade preferences set up by the Ottawa Agreement were, however, retained by the new South African Republic, and British and South African financial interests, particularly in the Rand, were not jeopardised. There followed several attempts in the General Assembly of the United Nations to bring about the expulsion of South Africa from that organisation, together with a boycott of her goods and a severing of diplomatic ties, but, so far, this has met with little success.

It now remains to be seen what further developments will take place in the south as a result of the break up of the Central African Federation and the problems arising from Rhodesia's unilateral declaration of independence.

11 South America—one of the areas of exploding population and great poverty. *Population in thousands* (1965):

Argentina	22,187	Colombia	15,434	Peru	11,854
Bolivia	3,668	French Guiana	36	Surinam	350
Brazil	88,200	Guyana	628	Uruguay	2,682
Chile	8,515	Paraguay	1,996	Venezuela	8,722

21 *The United States, Latin America and Cuba*

Since declaring themselves independent of Spain and Portugal during the Napoleonic War, the Latin American Republics have been of special interest to the United States. The Monroe Doctrine of 1823, which warned the world against interference in the western hemisphere, has become a jealously guarded principle of United States' foreign policy. Latin America has always been within the United States' sphere of influence, and for many years at the turn of the century, the United States Marines were regularly used to protect American interests in that area. Indeed, so bitter was Latin American reaction to this 'interventionism' that, despite Roosevelt's 'Good Neighbour Policy' initiated in the 1930's, and the post-war collaboration through the Organisation of American States, suspicion of the United States has by no means disappeared.

A *Post-war relations between the U.S.A. and Latin America:*

The growing need for mutual defence in the post-war world led to the Treaty of Rio de Janeiro in 1947, and to the principle that 'an attack against an American state is an attack against all', but the problems which arose from social injustice, economic exploitation and political tyranny in South America have not been so easily solved. The United States has given more than 2,500 million dollars in financial aid to South America since the Second World War, but much of it has been squandered by corrupt dictatorships or inefficient administrations.

At Santiago in Chile, in August 1949, the Foreign Ministers of the American States considered how democracy and social reform might be promoted in South America without infringing the principle of non-intervention, and a committee was set up to examine the causes of discontent in those areas where representative democracy did not exist. As a result of this committee's report and the work done on the subject at many inter-American conferences, there now seems to be a more concerted effort to impose collective sanctions upon oppressive tyrannies. Even so, the United States has not always had the support of all her South American allies in her attempts to deal with what she considers the serious threat of communism in Cuba.

In September 1960, Ministers from twenty American republics met at Bogota, Colombia, to discuss the effective measures which could be taken to further economic and social progress. It is significant that the United States government stated its belief that financial aid would not be sufficient to secure the southern hemisphere from communism. Money must be forthcoming, and an inter-American Development Bank was set up to administer it; but, as President Kennedy argued when asking Congress for some 600 million dollars to carry out United States' obligations under the Act of Bogota, there must be profound social changes in the South American Republics as well as economic development, because 'Full stomachs and lots of money in the bank or in the pocket of part of the population are not adequate defence against the communist lure.'

Concerted action in this direction took a big step forward at the Inter-American Economic and Social Council held at Punta del Este, Uruguay, in August 1961. It was there that the 'Alliance for Progress' was formed to seek equal opportunities for all in democratic societies. Plans were discussed which would stabilise prices, control disease, spread education amongst the masses, develop electric power and encourage investment in industry. The United States undertook to find some 20 billion dollars in ten years, in the hope that these ambitious schemes will transform the Latin American states into areas of stability and content. President Kennedy, however, gave his southern neighbours a fair warning. No United States' money would be forthcoming for any republic which did not agree to radical tax and land reforms, designed to further social justice and eliminate poverty.

It was hoped that if this 'great adventure of the Americas' succeeded, the western hemisphere would be freed from the menace of communism that Fidel Castro introduced into Cuba.

B *The Cuban revolution and the Castro régime:*

In its early days, Castro's revolution was nationalist and anti-American. Its task was to complete the work of Marti, whose revolution in 1895–1898 delivered Cuba from the political tyranny of Spain, only to leave her under the economic domination of the U.S.A. Castro was the heir of Marti, destroying the economic ties between Cuba and the United States, nationalising company after company in the name of absolute sovereignty. When the United States government retaliated by imposing certain sanctions on Cuba's trade, and later gave its blessing to the ill-fated and badly prepared invasion of the Bay of Pigs in 1961, Castro was able to justify his anti-American actions and win the sympathy of the Latin American republics who, as we have said, always tended to regard the United States with suspicion.

Some Latin American governments, in particular those of Brazil and Mexico, regarded the United States' attitude towards Castro's régime in Cuba as hypocritical. They saw the police state which has developed there and the acceptance of Russian aid as the natural reaction to a United States' policy which had remained quasi-imperialist and completely uncompromising. In this, however, they were not being strictly accurate, for the tyrannical nature of Castro's government was implicit in January 1959, when he came to power. The idea of the national will of the people being expressed at the Plaza by a show of hands—'The counter-revolution at home, the people with Fidel in the Plaza'—this exposed the government for what it was, an 'emotionally charged régime of the totalitarian left', as Raymond Carr described it in *The Observer*. Moreover, the socialisation of the economy was taken to such lengths that many of Castro's early supporters fled, their places being taken by known communists who, despite Castro's outburst against them in March 1962, were soon appointed to the main offices of state.

In 1961, Mr Dean Rusk, the United States' Secretary of State, claimed at Punta del Este that Castro's communism was imperilling the independence of all the western hemisphere, which the Organisation of American States was pledged to protect from foreign interference. In fact, this point of view carried the day, but it is interesting to note that the more democratic of the Latin American republics tended to argue that what happened in Cuba was a purely domestic affair and did not warrant interference from anyone. That this quite serious split in the Organisation of American States has now been healed, at least temporarily, was undoubtedly due to the introduction into Cuba of Russian offensive missiles.

C *The Cuban crisis:*

It was on Monday, October 22nd, 1962, that Mr Adlai Stevenson informed U Thant, the Acting United Nations' Secretary-General, that the Russians had installed missile bases in Cuba and that the United States intended to call an emergency meeting of the Security Council. Later that evening, President Kennedy announced that his government was instituting a naval blockade of Cuba, thus extending the United States–Russian conflict from the debating chambers of the United Nations on to the high seas. The next day, Stevenson tabled a resolution in the Security Council demanding the withdrawal of all offensive weapons from Cuba, a resolution which was unanimously endorsed by the Organisation of

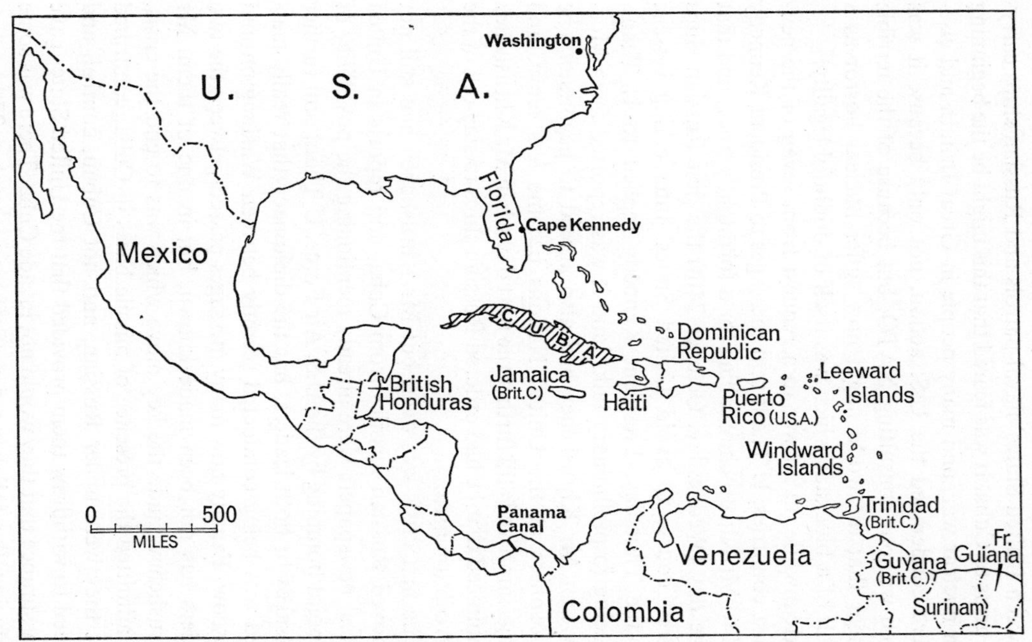

12 The proximity of Cuba to the U.S.A. and its potential influence in South America

American States, and the world waited for the expected clash between United States' naval patrols and Russian ships carrying arms to Cuba. It was feared that this might be the beginning of a nuclear war, and many people in Great Britain and elsewhere condemned the U.S. action, not only because it was taken without consulting NATO, but because of the terrible danger that the world might now suffer nuclear horror as a result of a blockade which was itself of doubtful legality.

Meanwhile, in answer to a request from seven of the neutralist countries, U Thant sent messages to President Kennedy and to Mr Khrushchev calling for a fortnight's truce, and that same day (Wednesday, October 24th) the first Russian ships altered course to avoid United States' intercepting vessels. On the Thursday, President Kennedy replied to U Thant, agreeing to preliminary talks, and it was reported from Moscow that Mr Khrushchev had also agreed to negotiate. The atmosphere at the United Nations became less tense, and things improved still further the next day when Mr Khrushchev announced that he had ordered Russian ships to stay out of the interception area.

The first crisis was over, but Mr Khrushchev had still not removed Russian missiles from Cuba, and reports in United States' newspapers were already mentioning the possibility of pinpoint bombing by the U.S. Air Force. U Thant sent further messages to both leaders, but the diplomacy that really mattered was being conducted secretly between Washington and Moscow. Exactly how many messages passed between the two leaders has not been made known, but in one of them, Mr Khrushchev made the key move which was to end the crisis. He admitted the presence of missile bases in Cuba, confirmed that they were under Russian, and not Cuban, control, and agreed to withdraw them provided that the United States gave an assurance that they would not invade Cuba. There was some confusion the following day (Saturday, October 27th) when

Moscow Radio announced that the Russian government would be willing to withdraw bases from Cuba if the United States dismantled her bases in Turkey. This proposal, however, was rejected by President Kennedy, and statesmen in many countries spent a tense Sunday morning awaiting confirmation of Mr Khrushchev's earlier promise. Meanwhile, the U.S.A. was preparing for direct military action against the bases.

Mr Khrushchev's reply came early on Sunday afternoon (G.M.T.). It was favourable, and the greatest crisis of the nuclear age was over.

D *The consequences of the Cuban crisis:*

The Cuban crisis brought about a re-examination of the balance of world forces:

1 The Chinese Communists claimed that the whole affair represented a 'Russian Munich', and the split between Moscow and Peking was widened when Mr Khrushchev reminded Mao Tse-tung that, though the imperialist powers might be 'paper tigers', they possessed 'nuclear teeth'. Mr Khrushchev, in fact, defended his compromise solution by pointing to the United States' promise not to invade Cuba. This, he stated, was his main object in putting the missiles into Cuba in the first place, and it is true that, though the United States government could revoke this part of the agreement on the grounds that Castro has refused to allow on-site inspection, it is unlikely that such a step will be taken.

2 From a military point of view, it would be well to recognise that the balance of forces involved in this particular crisis was undoubtedly tilted in favour of the United States. Not only was her nuclear striking-power superior to that of Russia, but the geographical position of Cuba gave the U.S.A. supremacy in conventional weapons, and the opportunity to force the Russian government to choose between

unleashing nuclear war or acceptance of United States' terms.

That the two leaders behaved in a calm and sensible manner throughout the crisis cannot be denied. By agreeing not to invade Cuba, President Kennedy allowed Mr Khrushchev to withdraw with dignity, and the United States government showed considerable wisdom in the moderate tones in which it accepted its victory. What was possible in Cuba might not be possible in Berlin, which is so much nearer to the U.S.S.R. than to the U.S.A.

3 As far as the United States' NATO allies were concerned, the Cuban crisis proved that when the two super-powers move to the brink of war, there is no time for consultation. This must have been particularly galling for Great Britain, whose independent nuclear deterrent failed to give her any voice in the development of the crisis. Indeed, Great Britain's 'special relationship' with the United States and the whole of NATO strategy was, once again, the subject of earnest discussion.

4 Lastly, the manner in which the United States government stood up to the threat of nuclear war had a sobering effect upon Russia, which, until the Cuban crisis, had tended to believe that the Kennedy administration would bow before any real threat to peace. From 1962 onwards, Mr Khrushchev knew exactly where he stood, and the danger of war from a miscalculation on his part was certainly decreased.

It was for this reason that some commentators soon began to speak optimistically about future United States–Russian relations. Both countries had come dangerously near to nuclear devastation; out of this could grow a more realistic approach to peaceful co-existence, though the bargaining would be hard and statesmen would need both patience and perseverance. (*For the events leading to the Partial Test Ban Treaty, see pages 43–45.*)

22 The British Commonwealth

A *The eighteenth and nineteenth centuries:*

Until a little more than a hundred years ago, the British Empire differed little from other empires of the past. It was composed of conquered territories and lands settled by colonists who had wished, for one reason or another, to leave the motherland. Its government was paternal in concept, though in the settled areas some progress had been made towards representative government. This provided an Executive, appointed by, and responsible to, the Crown, and a Legislature of two Houses, one wholly nominated by the Executive and the other elected by the colonists.

The first breach of this 'old colonial system' came with the American War of Independence (1776–1783) which shocked a complacent British government, quite unprepared for the revolutionary ideals of the day. The colonial reforms of William Pitt the Younger (1789–1801), succeeded in stabilising the position, at least for the time being, and it was not until 1837, when rebellion broke out in the provinces of Upper and Lower Canada, that the British Empire faced its next crisis. The Whig government at home then sent out Lord Durham to restore order and to report upon the political situation in the area. The report that bears his name is now acknowledged as one of the major turning-points in the transformation of a more or less orthodox Empire into the Commonwealth as we know it today.

Lord Durham suggested that in future, a Colonial Governor 'should secure the co-operation of the Assembly in his policy by entrusting its administration to such men as could command a majority', and he further stated that no aid from home should be expected 'in any difference with the Assembly that did not directly involve the relations between the mother country and the colony'. In brief, this meant self-government in all internal matters, and, though it was not immediately accepted by the British government, the idea began to take shape and soon this form of 'responsible government' spread throughout the settled colonies of the Empire.

Moreover, as the century progressed and the movement towards Federation developed, the new Dominions began to demand some control over their trade, foreign affairs and defence. In 1895 the Canadian government established a protective tariff in opposition to the recognised free-trade policies of the home government. In 1882 Great Britain, in making a commercial treaty with Montenegro, agreed that it should not, at that time, apply to any of the self-governing colonies, and in 1897 Great Britain renounced treaties with Belgium and Germany in order to permit the Canadian government to introduce a preferential tariff for British goods.

B *The First World War and the inter-war period:*

The right of the Dominions to control their own foreign policy and defence, however, did not come so easily. On August 4th, 1914, the British government was still in a position to declare war on behalf of all the Dominions, despite the claims to consultation which had been made at the turn of the century. At that time the growth of German power in the Pacific had been of great concern to the governments of Australia and New Zealand, and the British recognition of Germany's claim to Samoa angered them as much as the Anglo-French agreement over the New Hebrides in 1906. The Dominions felt that where their interests were directly involved, they should not only be consulted, but had the right to expect that their advice should be taken. In fact, however, it was not until the First World War loosened the ties which held the old world together that the Dominions gained recognition by the League of Nations as sovereign powers, and the Commonwealth emerged as a free association of nations, equal in status and united by a common allegiance to the Crown.

As a result of suggestions made at the Imperial Conferences of 1926 and 1930, the Parliament of Great Britain enacted the Statute of Westminster in 1931, which gave the force of law to what had, over the years, come to be accepted. This statute recognised the power of the Dominions to legislate with extra-territorial effect; it expressly stated that the British Parliament would never legislate for the Dominions without their consent, and it acknowledged that Great Britain had no right to hold up any Dominion legislation. The right of appeal to the Judicial Committee of the Privy Council was not immediately abolished, but the principle of total independence had been accepted and individual Dominions were now left to exercise their own choice in this matter.

At the outbreak of war in 1939, the new constitutional position of the Dominions was shown by their separate declarations of war, and, in the case of Eire, by its decision to remain neutral. Little further constitutional development was possible during the war years themselves, however, though the informal meeting of Commonwealth Prime Ministers in 1944 set a precedent which has been followed ever since.

C *Developments since the Second World War:*

The final stages of the evolution of the British Commonwealth began in the immediate post-war years:

1 The aim of self-government was not extended from the settled colonies to all dependent territories. This increased the potential membership of the Commonwealth, but it also raised other problems which might have destroyed a less flexible or resilient association.

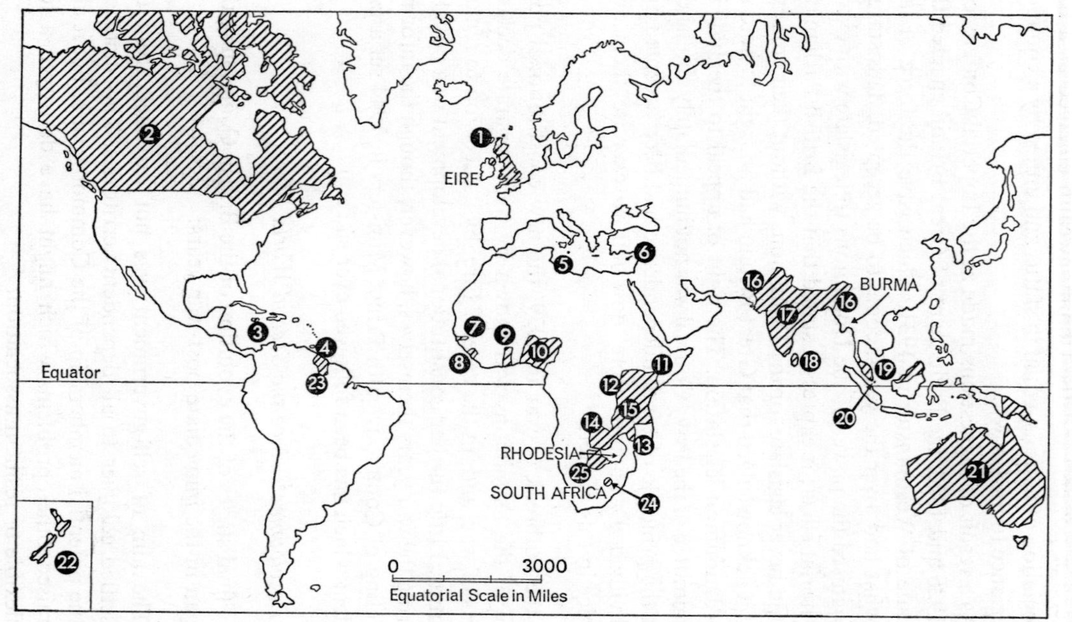

EIRE
BURMA
RHODESIA
SOUTH AFRICA
Equator
0
3000
Equatorial Scale in Miles
1
2
3
4
5
6
7
8
9
10
11
12
13
14
15
16
16
17
18
19
20
21
22
23
24
25

Some people have claimed that the fundamental social and political ideals which the original members cherished are no longer pursued by many newer members of the Commonwealth. Dictatorships have grown up which do not always heed the declaration of human rights, written into their constitutions on gaining independence, and this, in turn, has raised the question of whether the Commonwealth should expel those countries who depart from these principles. The decision to take such action over South Africa in 1961 presented such a test case, but men have since asked themselves whether this was done not so much on a question of principle, as to avoid the withdrawal of the Afro-Asian group who demanded it. There is the further argument that, so long as a country remains a member of the Commonwealth, it is always possible that other members will succeed in influencing its policies by persuasion in the intimate 'family' atmosphere of the Prime Ministers Conference. Once a member resigns or is expelled, this chance is lost.

---

opposite:

13 Countries of the British Commonwealth (excluding colonies and protectorates)

1 The United Kingdom
2 Canada
3 Jamaica
4 Trinidad & Tobago
5 Malta
6 Cyprus
7 Gambia
8 Sierra Leone
9 Ghana
10 Nigeria
11 Kenya
12 Uganda
13 Malawi
14 Zambia
15 Tanzania
16 E. & W. Pakistan
17 India
18 Ceylon
19 Malaysia
20 Singapore
21 Australia
22 New Zealand
23 Guyana
24 Lesotho
25 Botswana

a Guyana — independent 1966. Formerly British Guiana.
b Lesotho — independent 1966. Formerly Basutoland.
c Botswana — independent 1966. Formerly Bechuanaland.
d Eire — left Commonwealth in 1948.
e Burma chose to leave Commonwealth on gaining independence in 1947.
f Rhodesia declared independence unilaterally in 1965.
g South Africa — left Commonwealth in 1961.

The new Commonwealth also gives the impression to those who do not understand it, that it is more divided than ever on matters of defence and foreign policy. Some of the members belong to Western defence pacts, whereas others maintain a strict neutralism. Some are imbued with the Bandung spirit, whilst others have tended to be as suspicious of nationalism as they are of communism. This showed itself particularly at the time of the Suez crisis in 1956, when, for a short while, it seemed certain that a decisive rift in the Commonwealth would appear. Having overcome this crisis, however, and having heard the British government acknowledge the 'wind of change', there is now some hope that the Commonwealth will develop as a great multi-racial partnership, learning in a most cordial atmosphere how best to meet the many political, social and economic problems facing the world today.

2 When India became independent in 1947, she expressed a desire to become a republic and yet remain a member of the Commonwealth. This presented the Prime Ministers with a delicate constitutional problem, which they solved in 1949 by accepting India's request, it being understood that she would recognise the King (George VI) as Head of the Commonwealth, a symbol of a free association of states. Since then, India has been followed by Pakistan, Ghana, Cyprus, and Tanganyika and Zanzibar (Tanzania), and it is likely that other members of the Commonwealth will wish to follow a similar course.

3 Despite the fact that membership of the Commonwealth has increased since the war, countries have also won the right to withdraw from it. In 1947, the precedent was set by Burma. Speaking in the House of Commons at the time, the Prime Minister (Mr Attlee) gave the considered view of the British government of the day when he said, 'When, after due

consideration, the elected representatives of the people of Burma chose independence, it was, I believe, the duty of His Majesty's Government to take the necessary steps to implement their decision.' In 1949, Eire followed the same course, though with some reservations as to citizenship and trade.

D *The Commonwealth and the European Common Market (E.E.C.):*

There was some fear that the Commonwealth would begin to disintegrate if and when Great Britain entered the Common Market (*Chapter 23*). The British government made it clear in 1961–62 that certain economic safeguards would have to be provided for the Commonwealth trade with the mother country if the system of preferences was to be dismantled in favour of the common tariff of the E.E.C. Special consideration would have to be given to New Zealand, because her economic health depended almost entirely upon farm exports to the United Kingdom, but attention was also paid to cheap textile goods from India, Pakistan and Hong Kong, as well as to the primary produce of Australia. African states in the Commonwealth were to be offered association.

It has been said with some justification, however, that Great Britain's entry into the E.E.C. would have had a much wider effect upon the Commonwealth than was envisaged at the time of the negotiations. In January 1963, General de Gaulle vetoed British entry, because he claimed that the British people were not yet ready for it. He believed that they were not then willing to make the choice between their traditional 'blue water' Commonwealth interests and their geographical, cultural and economic ties with Europe. The British government had hoped to run a mean course between the two, but this, said de Gaulle, was illogical and impracticable. The choice may, even yet, have to be made.

23 The growth of the European Community: Britain and the Common Market

A *The idea of European unity:*

At the end of the Second World War, men everywhere began to turn their attention to the peace settlement and to the problems of preserving it. Many Europeans vowed that a new and united Europe must arise to prevent such a catastrophe from happening again, and their early post-war idealism was further strengthened by the growing fear of advancing Russian communism, which had already swept through eastern Europe and which took command of Czechoslovakia in 1948.

Many shades of opinion are to be found amongst those who advocated European union. *Laissez-faire* Liberals, who believed in free trade, allied with European Socialists, who believed that planning must be done on a supra-national scale. Statesmen who disliked the growing power of the U.S.A. and of Russia thought in terms of a European 'third force'—of resurrecting the Empire of Charlemagne, whilst many others, rejecting power and prestige as evils in themselves, wished to give a lead to the new nations of the world by surrendering nationalism when the latter were embracing it for the first time. Roman Catholics like Konrad Adenauer, de Gasperi and Robert Schuman worked alongside anti-clericals such as Guy Mollet and Henri Spaak in pursuit of a European Community.

In Great Britain, however, there was a more cautious approach. Though Churchill spoke in majestic terms about the European ideal, he was unable to stimulate much interest among the Conservative opposition, who could not forget their traditional foreign policy and their connections with the Empire and Commonwealth. Great Britain's Socialists also rejected the idea of a European Community. They feared that a loss of sovereignty would prevent them from adopting socialist policies peculiar to their own country, and they preferred to pin their faith on the United Nations as the only worthwhile international organisation. Thus, from the beginning, Great Britain remained outside the main stream of 'Community' thought, though the need for mutual defence and economic recovery forced British statesmen to negotiate with their European counterparts on such matters as the establishment of the Organisation for European Economic Co-operation (1948) to distribute Marshall Aid, and the setting up of the North Atlantic Treaty Organisation in 1949.

B *The Council of Europe:*

Meanwhile, at The Hague, a Congress of European statesmen met to discuss the calling of an Assembly of European parliamentarians. As a result of work done by men like Churchill, Ramadier, Adenauer, Reynaud and Hallstein, a Council of Europe met at Strasbourg in 1949, but its Consultative Assembly possessed no legislative powers and had no executive responsible to it. It did, however, provide a forum for discussion, and between 1949 and 1950 it pressed for the right to amend its constitution, seeking the establishment in Europe of a federal authority with minimal powers. This was rejected, first by representatives of the Labour government in Great Britain, and then by the Conservatives, who took office in 1951.

Obviously, no unanimous agreement could be reached on such an issue at Strasbourg, but there were other roads to European Union. One of these had been taken by Robert Schuman in 1950, when he suggested the pooling of European coal and steel resources under the direction of a high authority.

C *The Schuman Plan and 'the Six':*

It would be wrong to suggest that the Schuman Plan was inspired solely by progressive European ideas. The French

Foreign Minister at that time was undoubtedly worried by the danger of a German resurgence and by the problems that faced France in the Saar coalfields. His plan would give Europe the lead which it was seeking, and, at the same time, would bring to an end any potential Franco-German rivalry inherent in the economic miracle which was being worked in Germany. Once again, however, Great Britain showed her dislike of the idea. Mr Macmillan, speaking in the House of Commons at the time, said, 'One thing is certain and we may as well face it—our people will not hand over to any supra-national authority the right to close down our pits or our steel works'. Thus, only six nations ('the Six') met to draw up the treaty—France, Italy, Germany, Belgium, Luxembourg and the Netherlands. It was signed in 1951, and a High Authority, a Common Assembly, a Council of Ministers and a Court of Justice provided the institutions through which the common market in coal and steel was to be organised and administered.

Meanwhile, at the Council of Europe in Strasbourg, plans were being put forward by the Six which would result, sooner or later, in a full European Community. The Pflimlin Plan for agriculture was already being discussed in detail, so was a plan for a European transport community. When the Korean war caused the U.S.A. to press for a re-armed Germany, the creation of a European Union seemed to be very near indeed.

The history of the European Defence Community (E.D.C.), however, and the political organisation which, it was suggested, should go with it, proved that Europe was not yet ready—either for its own political constitution or for its own army, or even, at that time, for its own economic community.

On August 30th, 1954, a coalition of the Gaullist Right and the Communist Left prevented ratification of the E.D.C. by the French National Assembly. The French undoubtedly feared a new German Army, they felt that it would mean the end of their own military power, that it would weaken their political sovereignty and that it would lead to an economic community for which they were not, at that time, prepared. The fact that in December of the same year, the Western European Union was created, associating Great Britain with a new German Army and allowing the latter to join NATO, tends to prove that it was the political and economic implications of the E.D.C. which aroused suspicion in France at that time. In any case, the idea of European Union suffered a temporary check.

D *The Treaty of Rome and the establishment of the Common Market (E.E.C.):*

The momentum caused by the establishment of the coal and steel community was so great, however, that in 1955 the Six met again at Messina to take part in further discussions. Once again they chose the economic field in which to work, deliberately putting aside all questions of political sovereignty as beng too explosive for consideration at that time. They set up a ciommittee of experts under M. Spaak to explore ways of setting up a common market and of developing a European nuclear energy programme. This committee produced its report in April 1956. It suggested that, within twelve years, the customs barriers between the Six should be abolished and that a common external tariff should then surround them. This was to be the first step towards 'an even closer union' and was to be accompanied by the establishment of Euratom—the organisation for pooling nuclear resources.

The recommendations of M. Spaak's committee were accepted and, on March 24th, 1957, the Treaty of Rome was signed by the Six. This brought the European Economic Community and the Euratom Commission into existence on January 1st, 1958, and by early 1959 they had begun to function, leaving Great Britain, once more, isolated from the European movement.

E *The creation of EFTA:*

There can be no doubt that the British government at that time was faced with a most difficult problem. United States' capital was being transferred from London to the Continent, and news of economic expansion in the Common Market brought pressure from British firms, who felt that they had a lot to gain from free trade with Europe. It seemed that Great Britain would either have to seek a quick entry into the market after all or build something similar, either within the Commonwealth, or amongst the remaining nations of Europe. In fact, a White Paper was produced in July 1959, which suggested plans for the formation of a European Free Trade Association, and the agreement for this was signed in December of that year. EFTA, as it was called, included the United Kingdom, Norway, Portugal, Denmark and the three neutral states, Switzerland, Sweden and Austria.

It was felt that this association would provide British industry with a larger market for its goods, and that later it might act as a 'bridge' for opening negotiations with the Six. In effect, the creation of EFTA served to consolidate the Common Market, members of which, regarding Great Britain with the utmost suspicion, drew closer together and approved Hallstein's plan for 'accelerating' the timetable laid down in the Treaty of Rome.

F *Britain seeks entry into the Common Market:*

Thus it soon became clear that EFTA, which added only some 38 million people to the British home market, was a poor substitute for the exciting prospects which industry might enjoy within the Common Market and, in 1960, a significant change

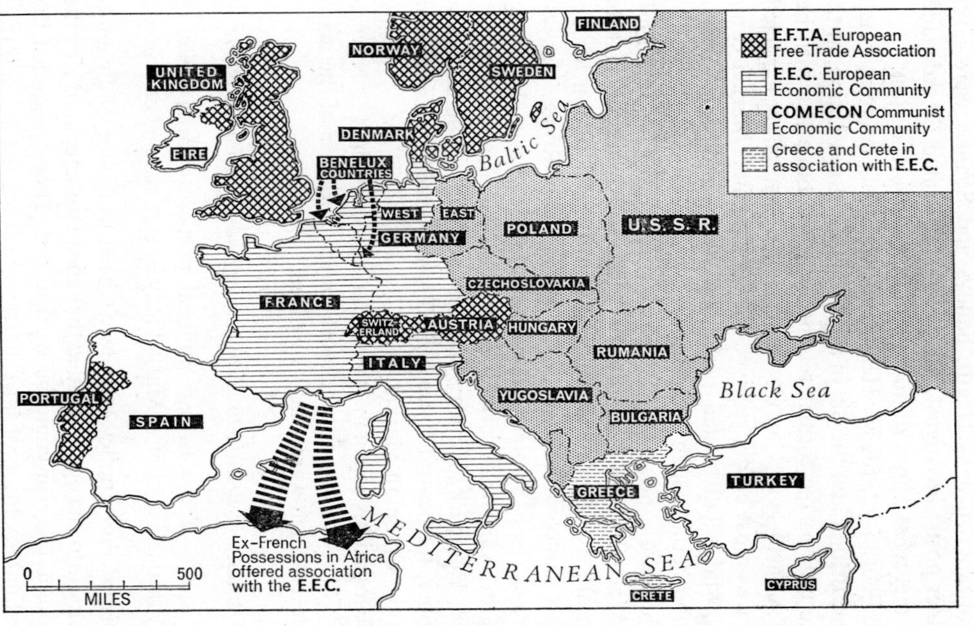

14 Economic alliances in Europe

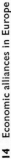

of British government policy became apparent. In June, 'good Europeans' such as Heath, Sandys and Soames were given cabinet posts; in August, Mr Macmillan visited Dr Adenauer and met what appeared to be a most cordial reception.

In February 1961, Mr Heath put forward a plan to associate Great Britain and the Six in a modified Customs Union, at the same time as the former retained her economic ties with her EFTA partners and her Commonwealth. As might be expected, this was most coldly received by the Common Market countries, who still distrusted 'perfidious Albion' and had no reason to offer her any such compromise.

The lesson, however, was quickly learnt, for, in July 1961, Mr Macmillan announced to the House of Commons that the government intended to seek entry into the Common Market in accordance with article 237 of the Treaty of Rome. This was approved by 313 votes to 5, with the Labour Party abstaining, and, in August, a formal application for membership was made. Denmark, Norway and Ireland followed suit, and, in October, the neutral states of EFTA also asked for association with the Common Market.

Negotiations began in earnest during the first half of November 1961, but proved to be most complex because of the many interests which were vitally involved.

G *Attitudes in Britain towards joining the Common Market:*

The views of the British political parties towards Britain's entry into the Common Market may be summarised as follows:

1 *Liberal Party* policy has always been in favour of Britain's entry into Europe, provided that adequate safeguards for the Commonwealth could be worked out. They applauded the gradual abolition of tariff barriers between the Six and they wanted Great Britain to play a full part in this new and exciting experiment in internationalism.

2 The *Labour Party* sat on the fence for a long time, but were given a more specific lead by Mr Gaitskell at their Conference in 1962. Then, and since, the official leadership of the party voiced its suspicions of the E.E.C. and left the British public in little doubt that its terms for joining the Six would be much more rigorous than those which the Conservative government seemed willing to accept in 1962–63. Labour Party criticisms of the E.E.C. included:

a The fact that it might become a 'rich man's club', maintaining a high external tariff to exclude cheap labour, intensive manufactures and agricultural produce from the developing countries, many of which are members of the British Commonwealth.

b A fear that their own plans for further socialisation of the British economy might be hindered by the closer association of Great Britain with the capitalist states of western Europe.

c A belief that the future development of western Europe might not be in the direction of true internationalism. There was a danger that it might enter world affairs as a 'third force'—in its own way as nationalistic as either the U.S.A. or Russia.

d When Great Britain surrenders her sovereignty, it must be to an organisation which would be certain to contribute towards the establishment of a world government.

3 The *Conservative Party* was not entirely united in favour of seeking entry into Europe, though the vast majority of its members acknowledged the economic advantages and accepted the Prime Minister's promise that the government would only join the Six provided that there would be reasonable safeguards for Commonwealth interests, for British agriculture and for the interests of Great Britain's EFTA partners—Norway, Sweden, Denmark, Portugal, Austria and Switzerland.

The British public in general naturally found it difficult fully to understand the significance of Great Britain's application to join the E.E.C. Major talking points, however, can be grouped under three headings, and some are given below:

1 *Economic:*

Could the growth of British industry be maintained if it were denied the expanding market of western Europe?

Is some sort of Commonwealth Association—i.e. a new and up-to-date Ottawa Agreement—a feasible alternative?

Could British farming survive the destruction of its system of deficiency payments and guaranteed prices, and compete favourably with its continental associates?

Would this not lead to a new revolution in British farming, comparable with that which had to be faced when the wheat-lands of Canada and the U.S.A. began to send their cheap produce across the Atlantic?

Would the free movement of labour, as laid down in the Treaty of Rome, affect employment and wage levels in Great Britain?

Would the common external tariff be gradually lowered to permit free trade with the rest of the world, including the United States, if the latter were willing to reciprocate?

2 *Political:*

How much sovereignty would be taken from the Parliament at Westminster if Great Britain were to join the Common Market?

Would the new Europe develop as a Federation of equal states, subordinate to a Federal Parliament at Strasbourg, or was it more likely that the *Europe des Patries* of President de Gaulle would be its ultimate form?

How far would the decisions of European bureaucrats,

sitting either in the Economic Commission, the High Authority (for coal and steel) or the Euratom Commission, interfere with daily lives in Great Britain, and what control would the British have over them?

3 *Psychological:*

Could the British people rid themselves of their traditional insularity?

Would they wish to associate more closely with their European neighbours?

Would it be a good thing that some purely British terminology and ideas should give way before European systems—e.g. the introduction of the decimal system, perhaps even the end of driving on the left-hand side of the road?

In short, do the British wish their future history to evolve within a European framework? Or is there an alternative?

H *The attitude of the United States:*

It was certain that the United States government favoured Great Britain's entry into Europe. President Kennedy felt that it would promote the unity and strength of NATO and remove the embarrassing claims made by the British government to a special relationship with the U.S.A. At the same time, a prosperous and contented Europe would be safe from communism and would be able to offer increased aid to the under-developed countries.

I *The attitude of the African territories:*

Amongst many of the newly independent English-speaking territories of Africa, there was considerable hostility towards the Common Market. Though they were offered association with the E.E.C. which would mean free entry into Europe for their exports, in exchange for the gradual reduction of their import duties (though exceptions would be made to protect infant industries), there was a feeling that this was a new attempt by the industrialised countries to impose their will upon the weaker, under-developed lands. This sentiment was summed up by President Nkrumah of Ghana, who said 'the creation of the E.E.C. as at present conceived will not only discriminate against Ghana and other independent states of Africa economically, but it will also perpetuate by economic means the many artificial barriers which were imposed on Africa by the European colonial powers.'

It was true that most of the French-speaking countries of Africa accepted association, but it is uncertain how far this is of permanent significance. At the moment, the French-educated African leaders are trying to preserve links with Europe and to promote association for economic reasons. Soon, however, these countries will begin to recognise the alternatives which political independence offers them and may wish to explore the possibilities of a Common Market in Africa.

J *The attitude of President de Gaulle—Britain's application is not accepted:*

In January 1963, it became obvious that President de Gaulle did not wish Great Britain to enter the E.E.C. at that time. At a press conference he announced that in his view, Great Britain was not yet ready to accept the Treaty of Rome and all that it stood for. He saw little point in prolonging the negotiations in Brussels, though he agreed that Great Britain might be offered some form of economic association with the Six.

This surprising development was not inconsistent with President de Gaulle's ideal of a united Europe, which he wanted to be independent of the U.S.A., free to follow its own foreign policy (possibly to the extent of a *rapprochement* with Russia,

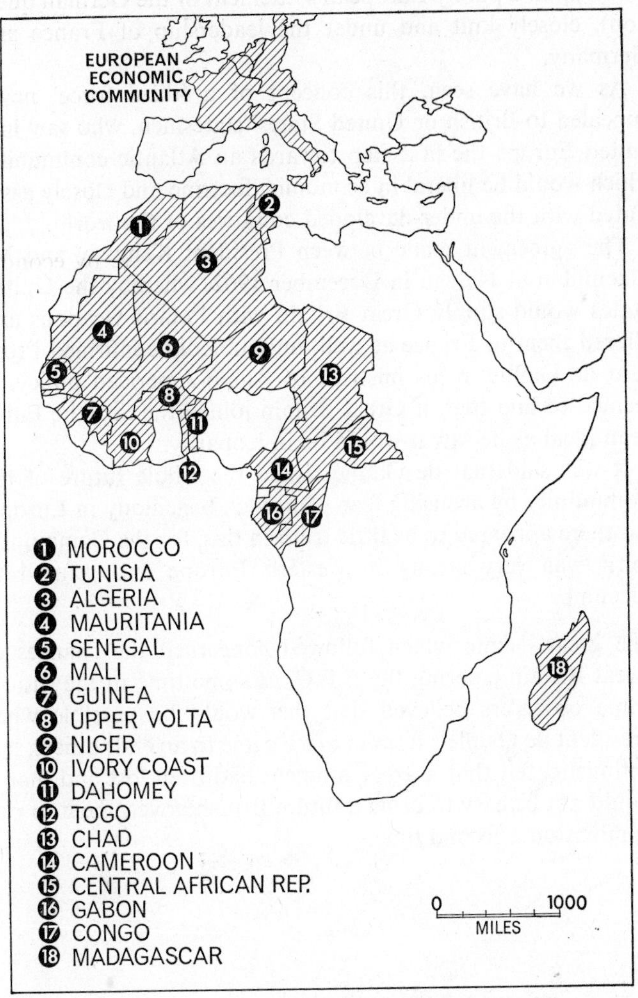

15 Ex-French African possessions. They are now states associated with the European Economic Community (E.E.C.)

based upon a purely European settlement of the German question), closely knit and under the leadership of France and Germany.

As we have seen, this concept of a 'third force' never appealed to British or United States' statesmen, who saw in a united Europe the first step towards an Atlantic community, which would be liberal in economic doctrine and closely associated with the under-developed countries of the world.

The agreement made between President Kennedy and Mr Macmillan at Nassau in December 1962, whereby the United States would supply Great Britain with Polaris weapons and offered them to France as well, undoubtedly confirmed President de Gaulle in his mistrust of Anglo-American policy. It seemed to him that, if Great Britain joined the Six, the European ideal as he saw it would be in jeopardy.

It was said that de Gaulle risked the whole future of the Community by arousing fear of French hegemony in Europe, but there appeared to be little truth in this, for the Community spirit was very strong in western Europe and refused to succumb.

The great debate which followed concerned the chances of Great Britain entering the E.E.C. at some time in the future. Some observers believed that this would be possible when President de Gaulle's term of office came to an end; others, less optimistic, felt that a great moment had been lost and that it would not be easy to bring a future British government to risk humiliation a second time.

24 Summit meetings 1959-1960

A *The Camp David meeting:*

Two factors of major importance in world affairs led to the temporary relaxation of tension attributed to the Eisenhower–Khrushchev meeting at Camp David in September 1959:

1 The death of the American Secretary of State, Mr John Foster Dulles, permitted a more flexible approach to world problems on the part of the Eisenhower administration. It has been written 'Eisenhower with Herter as his Secretary of State appeared to be a different man from Eisenhower with Dulles', and there can be no doubt of the accuracy of this statement. Dulles had been guided by a rigid set of principles. For him, there could be no negotiated settlement with communism, which was evil of itself and would burn the fingers of anyone who attempted to come to terms with it. Thus, ideas of disengagement in Europe were anathema to him and he made no attempt to conceal his disapproval of Mr Macmillan's approaches to Moscow in early 1959.

2 It was beginning to dawn upon both Washington and Moscow that the two greatest powers in the world were so far in advance of their neighbours from the military point of view that, whether they liked it or not, the future of the world really rested upon decisions taken by them. Obviously, they would want to consult their allies (and people in Great Britain liked to feel that they had a special relationship with the U.S.A. by virtue of their possession of the hydrogen bomb), but they alone had to face the responsibility of taking the greatest decisions. It is not surprising, therefore, that in 1959 Eisenhower and Khrushchev agreed to visit each other's country. This was merely a recognition of the new distribution of power in the mid-twentieth century.

The climax of Mr Khrushchev's visit to the U.S.A. in 1959 was undoubtedly his meeting with President Eisenhower at Camp David. The spirit of compromise which seemed to come from this meeting of the two leaders was held to be proof that Mr Khrushchev had scrapped the Leninist hypothesis that war between communism and capitalism is inevitable. Here was the supreme triumph of the ideal of peaceful co-existence, and further developments in this direction could be expected when an official Summit Meeting had been arranged and when President Eisenhower paid his visit to Russia in 1960.

Looking back upon the Camp David meeting, of course, it is now easier to understand that too much was expected of it. The language difficulty was immense and undoubtedly accounted for Mr Khrushchev's belief that President Eisenhower would compromise on Berlin. The atmosphere was relaxed and friendly, but nothing was committed to paper. The leaders seemed to be getting on well together and people were soon talking about the 'Camp David spirit', but, in reality, nothing of substance had changed. The differences between East and West were still there, and it seems that both Eisenhower and Khrushchev deceived themselves if they ever seriously thought that the road towards peaceful co-existence would now be an easy one. Nevertheless, no communist leader has ever spoken with such warmth towards any western statesman as did Mr Khrushchev on his return to Russia in 1959–60.

The world was led to believe that at long last, a real *détente* was possible, and preparations went ahead for the final Summit Meeting, to be held in May 1960 at the Palais de Chaillot in Paris. This, however, was not to come about.

B *The 'U2' incident and its consequences:*

On Wednesday afternoon, May 18th, 1960, Mr Khrushchev declared, in a most histrionic manner, that all hopes of a settlement between East and West were premature. At his press conference that afternoon he ranted and raved against 'American Aggressors' in a personal performance lasting over two and a half hours. Much has been written to explain the true significance of this dramatic change; fundamentally, all agree that Mr Khrushchev considered that his 'friend' of Camp David had betrayed him by ordering the flights of United States' reconnaissance aircraft (known as U2's) over Russian territory.

On May 1st, 1960, a specially designed plane, piloted by Mr Gary Powers and under the direction of the Central Intelligence Agency, took off on an espionage-cum-photographic mission from a base in Pakistan. It did not return, and on May 5th, Mr Khrushchev announced to the Supreme Soviet in Moscow that a United States' plane, caught deep within Russian air space, had been shot down. There followed a series of contradictory announcements from the United States government, culminating in the statement of May 6th that 'there was absolutely no—NO—deliberate attempt to violate Soviet air space . . . and never had been'. All that remained for Mr Khrushchev to do was to produce Gary Powers and the equipment which had fallen into Russian hands, including part of the U2 aircraft itself. This he did, and the United States' humiliation was complete. Not only had her government been caught out in a flagrant breach of faith, but, even when President Eisenhower was given a chance to 'save face' by denying responsibility for the incident, he failed to seize it. The impression gained was certainly one of a tired administration, incapable of wrestling with the complex tasks of the modern world, and of a President not really in command of his own government agencies—a nice man caught up in a turmoil of international immorality.

Some observers expressed surprise that Mr Khrushchev should take such an indignant stand against this simple act of aerial espionage. The western press compared this with the incredible efficiency of Russian spy organisations in the United States. They sometimes failed to point out, however, that the Russian government had now learnt, for the first time, just how much the United States knew of its military installations and industrial distribution. When one considers that the nuclear balance was still acknowledged to be in favour of the U.S.A., that Russia has a tradition of secrecy and a dread of interference, that fear of war and distrust of the United States is always uppermost in Russian minds, and that Mr Khrushchev's policy of co-existence had never been acceptable to the Chinese and even to some of his own colleagues, we can understand more easily why the Russian leader showed such a remarkable degree of bad temper when he learnt that the U2 had been shot down.

Whichever way the West looked at this incident, it was impossible to disagree with Mr Walter Lippman's view that the inept handling of the affair by the United States government 'transformed the embarrassment of being caught in a spying operation into a direct challenge to the sovereignty of the Soviet Union'.

25 The United Nations Organisation

The idea of a United Nations Organisation, based upon the sovereign equality of member states and the continued co-operation of the United States and Russia, was not the original intention of Churchill and Roosevelt during the early years of the Second World War.

At first, both men felt that a system of Regional Groups, held together by a Great Power Triumvirate, would be more successful. Churchill in particular, realising the growing weakness of Great Britain relative to the other members of the Grand Alliance, worked especially hard to secure its continuation into the post-war world. At the same time, he did all he could to build up a 'special friendship devoid of sinister intent' with the United States of America. In his 'Morning Thoughts' (February 1943) he envisaged three Regional Councils (in Europe, in the Pacific and in the western hemisphere) over which would stand the Supreme World Council, made up of the victorious powers of the Grand Alliance, supported by members of the Regional Councils, sitting in rotation.

There were many arguments against the Churchillian plan for the post-war world, however, and these were voiced not only in Moscow but in the Western capitals as well. Mr Cordell Hull feared that Regionalism might bring about the return of United States' isolationism in the western hemisphere. Some British statesmen argued that it would lead to the rise of power blocs, and others seemed uncertain whether the United States and Russia would allow Great Britain to be a member of all Regional Councils, as Churchill hoped. It must be remembered that the U.S.A. and Russia were then united in their opposition to colonialism. Finally, it was said that Regional Groups would lead to the formation of closed trade areas, and this ran counter to economic thought at that time.

A *First steps towards the establishment of UNO:*

The argument was brought to an end in October 1943, by the Moscow Declaration, which opened the way for detailed discussion on the establishment of a General International Organisation. On the whole, public opinion welcomed this with enthusiasm, though it was never so vocal in Great Britain as it was in the U.S.A. British people were happy to know that the great powers would continue to co-operate with each other in the post-war world, but British statesmen were still preoccupied with the problems arising from the relative decline of British power. In January 1944 Lord Halifax appealed for closer Commonwealth political unity, to allow Great Britain to negotiate on terms of equality with her allies; but this met with a poor response from Commonwealth countries, who were jealous of their independence, and provoked Russia to claim the admission of all her sixteen republics to the new United Nations Organisation if a Commonwealth bloc emerged.

Meanwhile, discussions had begun at Dumbarton Oaks, and in October 1944, proposals were put forward outlining the shape of the future organisation. There was to be a Security Council and a General Assembly, but it was to be the former which would be charged with maintaining world peace, in accordance with the principles of the Charter.

B *The Security Council and the problem of the veto:*

The Security Council was to be composed of the great powers and six non-permanent members (including one from the British Commonwealth). It could debate only questions of security and was precluded from discussing domestic disputes, and, though it was to be in continuous session, ordinary processes of diplomacy were protected by the proviso that all parties should first seek to solve disputes by negotiation.

The question that still had to be answered, however, concerned the method by which the Security Council should take its decisions. At first, Great Britain wished to preclude a great power who was party to a dispute from voting, either on enforcement measures or on suggestions for a pacific settlement. After some hesitation, the United States agreed with this, but Russia insisted on the unanimity of the great powers before action could be taken or suggestions made. Thus, rather unceremoniously, the delegates framing the organisation were brought face to face with the fundamental problem: Was the United Nations to be a device through which the great powers would act to rule the world, or was the Charter of the United Nations to become a body of law which would be above even the great powers?

Judged from a distance, both these possibilities seem unrealistic, but in 1944 the great powers were acting together to defeat Germany, and the idea of a *pax suprema* in the post-war world was not easily discarded. Moreover, some British diplomats soon realised that Great Britain herself might need the veto in face of the anti-colonialism of both the United States and Russia. They had to weigh this factor carefully against the dismay which would be felt in Britain's Dominions by the establishment of a great-power oligarchy.

In the event, a compromise was reached at Yalta in January 1945, which provided that, though no great power could be subjected to enforcement, it could not prevent discussion of a dispute to which it was a party. Moreover, the Security Council could recommend peaceful solutions and call upon parties to use them, though every member of the Security Council had an unqualified right to prevent the Council from determining whether there was a threat to peace or an act of aggression. This formula, of course, left the great-power veto largely intact, but it was realistic and comforting to all the governments of the great powers, who had been thinking deeply on the subject during the latter part of 1944.

During this period, discussions had also been held about the feasibility of setting up an International Armed Force. Great Britain proposed a United Nations Military Staff Committee, which might organise sanctions and military armaments. The United States added proposals for 'special agreements' by which states would put some of their armed forces at the disposal of the United Nations, and Russia suggested an International Air Force. All these proposals were built into Articles 42 and 43 of the Charter, but, though some effort was made to put them into practice in 1945–46, a United Nations World Force has not yet materialised, and the Security Council has only been able to 'recommend' military action, never to 'call upon' members to take part in it.

In April 1945, forty-five nations met at San Francisco to engage in final discussions on the establishment of a United Nations Organisation. The right of permanent members of the Security Council to a veto was extended to cover applications for admission, and a code of eligibility was laid down, which demanded that new states should be peace-loving and willing to accept and carry out the principles of the Charter.

Because of the system of majority voting in the General Assembly, permanent members of the Security Council have tended to veto the admission of states who might vote in opposition to their general policy, and, on this matter, members of the United Nations have often shown disapproval of the United States policy which made entry into the United Nations depend upon support for the West in the 'cold war'. Some neutrals have contrasted this attempt to turn the United Nations into an anti-communist club, with the more flexible 'package' proposals of Russia, which sought to preserve the balance of forces in the organisation.

C *The General Assembly and the 'Uniting for Peace' machinery:*

Though the Security Council retained whatever executive authority remained within the United Nations Organisation (bearing in mind the veto), the General Assembly, with its right of discussion and recommendation, has become a world forum where 'peaceful change' can be initiated and debated. Those states whose interests lie in the preservation of the *status quo* have often found this an embarrassment, but as the years have gone by, the General Assembly has increased in value as an instrument for assessing world opinion.

Moreover, in November 1950, the 'Uniting for Peace' resolution which the General Assembly passed by fifty votes to five, with two abstentions, increased the actual powers of that body in the maintenance of peace. The resolution affirmed that, should the Security Council fail to exercise its authority, the Assembly was to consider any threat to peace, and was even to recommend the use of force if necessary. An emergency session should be held within twenty-four hours on the vote of any seven members of the Security Council, or if a majority of the Assembly indicated that that was their wish. A Peace Observation Commission was to be established and United Nations' observers were to be sent to troubled areas. Further measures were also suggested. Members were invited to survey their resources and to keep a mobile force ready for service with the United Nations, whilst a Collective Measures Committee was set up to study all methods of strengthening peace and security.

Though not all these reforms have been fully implemented, the 'Uniting for Peace' machinery has been used effectively on several occasions since its inception—the best known being 'Suez' and 'Hungary' in 1956 and the 'Congo' in 1960.

D *Article 51 of the U.N. Charter:*

A word must be said about Article 51 of the Charter, which

gives each member-state the right to take measures of individual and collective self-defence against armed attack until the Security Council is able to take over. This article was inserted, not only to cover the interval between an act of aggression and action by the Security Council, but also as a safeguard against disagreement within the Security Council which might preclude any action whatsoever from being taken. Some states, indeed, had so little confidence in the United Nations that, from the beginning, they looked to regional defence organisations as the only worthwhile forms of protection. Under this 'escape clause' such defence agreements as NATO, SEATO and the Baghdad Pact were negotiated, though the Sino-Soviet Treaty of 1950 and all the Russian treaties with eastern European countries were signed under Article 107 of the Charter, which allows regional groupings against ex-enemy states.

Article 51, however, applies only in the event of armed aggression, and then only until the Security Council has taken the necessary steps to restore peace—an unlikely event since the break-up of the Grand Alliance. This has ensured that the defensive purposes of the Western defence pacts will always predominate and that NATO, for example, can never be used as an instrument for the liberation of eastern Europe.

E *UNO and the League of Nations:*

The successes and failures of the United Nations have inevitably been compared with those of its predecessor, the League of Nations; but, whereas the League was created in an atmosphere of idealism which reflected the shock administered by the horrors of the First World War upon a people unprepared for it, the creators of the United Nations never allowed their hopes to blind them to the realities of the world situation.

In 1919, and earlier, such men as Dr Gilbert Murray, Viscount Cecil and President Wilson could only explain the outbreak of the First World War in terms of a breakdown of the traditional diplomatic methods. They still believed that nations, as well as men, were naturally full of goodwill and that all disagreements could be solved if certain moral principles were followed and if 'open covenants' were 'openly arrived at'. This new diplomacy survived the disillusionment of the 1930's and found its champions amongst the leading statesmen of the U.S.A. at San Francisco in 1945. In fact, however, owing to the nature of the 'cold war', open diplomacy often turned into 'diplomacy by insult'. Governments uttered high-sounding phrases to cloak their real intentions, because they needed to placate domestic opinion or wished to win support from the uncommitted nations. Any settlement between the two great power blocs had to be carefully prepared in the lobbies of the United Nations, or even in their respective embassies, before it came to the United Nations for endorsement. Thus the diplomacy of the future may well be 'open covenants' privately arrived at, a compromise which perhaps offers the best chance of success.

F *UNO as a World Forum:*

The establishment of Regional Defence Organisations helped to stabilise the position of the powers in the 'cold war', and allowed any new conflict to come to the front at the United Nations. The post-war era witnessed the gradual contraction of European colonial power, but for some, particularly for the Bandung powers, assisted by the Latin American bloc, the movement towards national independence was not progressing fast enough. The General Assembly provided these powers with a world forum where they could not only work to speed up this process, but were able to deliver impassioned speeches against the very concept of imperialism. In 1947, the Egyptian delegate stated 'we are here to challenge the basic assumptions of nineteenth-century imperialism', and Great Britain, as well as the other colonial powers of the West, has been subject to pressures in the United Nations which have been met only by resorting to Article 2 (7) of the Charter, defining the scope of domestic jurisdiction. Great Britain conceded that the United Nations Organisation was entitled to intervene if there was a genuine threat to international peace, but she claimed that the internal tranquillity of an overseas territory remained the responsibility of the sovereign power. This has been challenged many times by members quoting Article 55, which deals with human rights, or Article 14, which empowers the General Assembly to 'recommend' measures for the adjustment of any situation, regardless of origin. Great Britain, however, has always answered that human rights have never been defined in law, whilst Article 14 refers only to any international situation which might arise between sovereign states.

It is felt in some quarters that the United Nations has been a useful safety-valve where Afro-Asian nationalists could release much of the bitterness they felt towards those European powers who dominated them for so long; but there was always the danger that, if the latter were too hard-pressed, they would reconsider their attitude towards the organisation. France, indeed, did walk out of the Assembly over the question of Algeria, and on one occasion when Cyprus was debated, Great Britain let it be known that she might refuse to co-operate. In the 1960's, however, only the last vestiges of European dominance remain, and it is now possible that the new nations will turn their attention to the study of Sino-Soviet imperialism, which has so far escaped their lash.

26 A Decade of Development: the 1960's

In December 1961, the General Assembly of the United Nations unanimously adopted a resolution designating the 1960's as the 'United Nations Development Decade', and in May 1962 U Thant, then Acting Secretary-General of the United Nations, speaking in Copenhagen, said, 'A new freedom stares the wealthy nations in the face—the freedom to help or not to help their neighbours who still lie on the far side of abundance and who do not yet command the means to help themselves.'

A *The world in the 1960's:*

1 Inequality:

a At least two-thirds of the world's present population does not eat enough to preserve good health. Only 20–25 per cent of the world's population regularly receives the necessary 2,200 calories each day.

b It often happens that where the population density is greatest, the amount of food available is at its lowest. Thus, over 70 per cent of the underfed people of the world are concentrated in Asia, and a further 18 per cent live in Africa and Latin America.

c There is a growing gap between the living standards in the developed and under-developed countries of the world. In the former, annual incomes range from £200 to far above £1,000; in the latter, they average as little as £25 per year. Moreover, the population living in developed countries can look forward to a doubling or trebling of their standards of living within the foreseeable future, whereas, because of the increase in population, the standards of living in many under-developed countries—particularly in

Asia—are falling. In other words, living standards in some countries are lower in the 1960's than they were a generation ago. This can be better understood when it is realised that, although by the mid-1950's world food production had risen by 8 per cent over the pre-war figure, the world's population had risen by at least 14 per cent. It has also been calculated that in the 1940's only half the world's population was undernourished, whereas now a conservative estimate is two-thirds.

2 The population explosion:

a During the past two hundred years a medical and sanitary revolution has totally eliminated many diseases and has taught men how to control others. Infant mortality has fallen at such a rate that nowadays six babies out of every seven who would have died two centuries ago are saved. At the same time the knowledge of medicine which the developed countries have slowly acquired has now suddenly become available elsewhere. Thus, for example, the malarial mosquito in Ceylon has been exterminated by DDT, with the result that the death rate fell from 22 to 12 per thousand in seven years. The medical revolution has also raised the general level of health in those areas where people have been subject to all sorts of tropical diseases, and this increase in vigour has now led to an increased birthrate in those areas of about 30,000 a year—twice the rate ever experienced in Europe.

b Each day, the population of the world increases by 88,000, that is, by thirty-four million people a year. Moreover, since the rate of increase is greater now than it was a decade ago, it is expected that the present world population of under 3,000 million people will have reached 3,600 million by 1980. There can be no doubt that during the next few years, man's ingenuity will be taxed to the full in an effort to prevent starvation from undoing all the good that the medical revolution has achieved.

3 The effects of travel, radio, transport, etc.:

Improvements in communications, education and travel (particularly during the war), have enabled people in the under-developed countries to learn how the rich part of the world lives. They are now no longer content with their lot in life: they have learned that it is possible not only for individuals to be rich, but for whole societies to attain a high degree of affluence. This is where the humane and political aspects of the problem are seen to merge, for every political leader in Africa, Asia and Latin America must promise his people higher standards of living quickly, and the appeal of Russia, which has achieved a high degree of industrialisation in forty years, is most attractive to backward peoples. Those who have lived so close to death remain unmoved when the West points to the cost in personal freedom which the Russian citizen has had to pay for the achievements of his state. Indeed, it is with this in mind that we watch with great interest the development of India and China. If the former fails in her efforts to reconcile political freedom with speedy economic growth, then the communist system will have won a vital victory in the 'cold war'.

B *Problems facing the under-developed countries:*

1 The capital assets of under-developed countries are too inadequate to allow for the growth of industry, and without financial help they are not likely to improve, because their governments lack the capital necessary for investment in new roads, railways, land reclamation, irrigation and mineral exploitation. Many economists believe that unless a country can invest at least 12 per cent of its national income in development schemes, it will never reach a point from which

it can begin to grow of its own volition. It seems likely that few, if any, of the under-developed countries have reached this position yet.

2 According to classic economic theory, increased production depends upon increased investment in capital, labour and land, but figures for the United States, Russia, Great Britain, Mexico, etc., prove that production increases at a much greater rate if additional investment is put into human resources, i.e. into education, health, skills, teaching by mass-media, and so on. Here the under-developed countries are at a grave disadvantage, for their people are often illiterate, they lack even the most rudimentary industrial skills and, as they assume political independence, there is the danger that in the first flush of extreme nationalism, they may alienate the few managers, administrators, teachers, etc. who have remained with them after the withdrawal of the imperial power.

3 In 1948 a report from the Colonial Development Corporation estimated that a project carried out in a backward area cost twice as much as it would do in a developed country with water supplies, good road and rail services, communications, electric power and all other necessary services. Thus the need for financial aid becomes imperative if the United Nations ambition to raise the annual rate of growth in the under-developed countries from 3 to 5 per cent is to be realised by 1970. In fact, aid to Asia, Latin America and Africa will have to increase from the present 500 million dollars a year to over a billion by 1970.

4 Financial grants and loans are certainly a vital need of the under-developed countries in the 1960's, but they also require to expand their trade with the developed countries if they are ever to stand securely upon their own feet. Aid may help them in their period of development, but unless they

can repay what they have borrowed, and unless they can rid themselves of their dependence upon primary agricultural products (which always fall in price before anything else), they are unlikely to become truly independent.

5 There are also, of course, the physical difficulties which face the under-developed countries. It has been estimated by a United Nations' agency (1954) that potential crop land in the world covers 4,000 million acres. We know that four-fifths of this is in fact already under cultivation. Of the uncultivated fifth, the F.A.O. has estimated that one-third lies in Asia, a quarter in North and Central America (Canada in particular), a quarter in Africa, and not much elsewhere. Moreover, not only does this land sometimes lie far from centres of great backward populations, but it also presents certain problems as far as development is concerned:

a The land may be very difficult to clear.

b Much of the land is at present desert, and will remain so until great irrigation schemes have been put into effect.

c Pests and diseases have to be attacked in many areas before people can be expected to farm them.

d The work will have to be done by hard-working and skilled farmers, and these are not easily found even where investment in education is at its highest. Time is also needed to break down traditional ways of life, for peasants tend to be conservative and refuse to accept change. But time is not available, for even if the new lands could be brought into cultivation immediately, their products would not be sufficient to match the demands of the rapidly growing world population.

6 The whole question of population control is, of course, extremely complex, and is made worse by the fact that there is always a considerable time-lag between the fall in death rates and the fall in birth rates. From the start of the medical revolution in the United Kingdom, it took 130 years before the population became more or less stable. Moreover,

though governments have actively promoted means of death control, they have nearly always refused to take action in the matter of birth control. The latter has now become acceptable in most of the developed countries (despite Roman Catholic opposition) but, except in India, has found little support elsewhere. Population growth is consequently greatest in backward countries and is contributing to the growing inequalities between rich and poor people mentioned in 'A' above.

C *What the developed countries can do to help:*

1 There must obviously be an enormous increase in financial aid to backward countries. So far, this has taken various forms. Most of it has been in the form of bi-lateral agreements between governments or by private investment, and various observers have argued for or against an extension of this method. It is obvious that mother countries have tended to give aid to their colonies or ex-colonies, because they feel that they have a special relationship with them; against this, there is the feeling amongst many backward peoples that these agreements only delay their movement towards independence in the fullest sense. Thus, efforts are now being made to direct more financial aid through the various multilateral agencies which exist—the World Bank, the International Development Association and the European Economic Community, for example. Even here, however, distinctions have to be made, for, with the development of the E.E.C. and its communist rival COMECON, there is a danger that the international agencies of the United Nations may be forced to take a back seat as East and West compete more vigorously to win over the uncommitted countries. Some people feel that if all aid could be channelled through the United Nations, that organisation would attain such a

standing in world affairs that it might become the basis of a world authority.

There is a further complication regarding increased aid to developing countries. This concerns the rates of interest, for it must be remembered that much aid takes the form of short- or long-term loans negotiated on a business basis. Thus the 'credit worthiness' of a country is always taken into account before aid is given, and there is a definite danger that borrowing at commercial rates of interest may saddle a developing state with an impossible repayment problem during the years ahead.

This is illustrated by the example of India, where, after borrowing at normal rates of interest—i.e. 5 per cent—she now finds herself trying to pay off a debt amounting to approximately 400 million dollars a year, or 25 per cent of her export earnings. She has now entered into her third five-year plan and has borrowed more money, which means that an even higher percentage of her export earnings will be earmarked for debt-servicing for many years to come.

It is obvious, therefore, that a new approach to lending must be introduced in the 1960's, and in this the International Development Association shows the way. Through this organisation, it is now possible to secure a fifty-year loan with no interest payment, and with repayments of capital increasing slowly after the first ten years. This type of loan was negotiated by the Indian government before undertaking the Damodar Valley scheme, and observers believe that it will set the pattern for borrowing in the 'Decade of Development'. At the moment, however, funds available to the International Development Association only amount to 150 million dollars a year—or 2·5 per cent of the amount needed annually.

2 So far, grants and loans have usually been tied to particular

projects. This means that work can proceed with a minimum of inspection, and it is possible to view the results when the job is done. This has, however, caused inflationary tendencies to appear in the economies of backward countries, for a project requires labour, and labour implies consumption. Unless, therefore, the amount of consumer goods, especially agricultural produce, can be increased to meet this additional demand, prices will rise. There can be little doubt that aid during the 1960's must include aid to produce consumer goods, as well as capital goods. This will raise practical difficulties of inspection, and will require patience and understanding on the part of the donor countries.

3 Apart from capital, there are other forms of aid now being investigated:

a It is obvious that food output per head of the population is growing in western Europe at about twice the rate of growth of the population. This means that, in the 1960's, western Europe, as well as the U.S.A., will have a surplus of foodstuffs. Somehow or other, this food will have to be directed to the backward peoples who need it, and farmers will have to be protected by international commodity agreements guaranteeing prices for a definite period of time.

b As we have seen (*see* B4), developing countries will wish to free themselves from a total reliance upon primary produce, but it is certain that their first attempts at industrialisation will demand 'labour intensive capital equipment'. Much of this has become obsolete in the West, where labour is very expensive, and a Swedish businessman, Mr Langenskold, has already set up an organisation to send second-hand machinery to backward countries. This scheme may well be extended, with the developed countries sending technicians for servicing the plant and for teaching others how to do so.

c The sending of trained personnel is another form of aid which is vital to the developing countries. To achieve an annual average increase of 5–6 per cent in their gross national products, it is estimated that the developing countries will have to expand their skilled human resources by 300–400 per cent during the Decade. To tackle this problem, conferences have already been held in Addis Ababa, Santiago and Tokyo. There, Ministers of Education discussed how 'to take the necessary steps to devote to education the maximum economic resources available' and to make the best use of external aid to Africa, Latin America and Asia. UNESCO is also to inaugurate a World Campaign against Illiteracy and is working in close contact with the developing countries upon this project. It is intended that by 1970 these countries should themselves invest between 4 and 5 per cent of their gross national product in education.

4 Trade:

Increased trade between the developed and the developing countries is perhaps the most vital objective sought by the United Nations during the Decade of Development. If this is achieved, growth will be permanent and dignified, loans will be repaid on time and in full, and results beneficial to both sides will be brought about. To achieve an increase in trade sufficient to be of any real value, a new pattern of world trade has been suggested:

a Many economists feel that a giant free-trade area, covering all rich nations, must be established. To this area, the backward countries must be allowed to sell not only primary products, but simple industrial products such as textiles.

b At the same time, the rich countries must not expect similar free-trade benefits to be extended to them by the developing countries, because if this came about the demand for imports by the people of these countries would be so great that it would outweigh exports. Thus, instead of being strengthened, these countries would find themselves with an adverse balance of payments, which would grow worse year by year.

This development in world trade has already been furthered by the work of GATT, which has ordered an increase in the quotas governing imports of cheap labour intensive manufactures into the rich countries of the world. In this matter the United Kingdom has a most impressive record. President Kennedy also suggested further plans to be adopted by the United States and the E.E.C. together. They include:

(i) The abolition of all duties by the United States and the E.E.C. on all goods in which they do 80 per cent of the world's trade.
(ii) A reduction in, or the elimination of, duties on tropical foodstuffs.
(iii) A reduction by up to 50 per cent on all the rest.

If this comes about, a great step will have been taken to assist the developing countries towards economic independence. There can be no doubt, however, that such a unilateral freeing of trade will cause hardship to the rich. Already, in the United Kingdom, textile companies have complained of growing competition in the home market from Hong Kong, Pakistan and India. Again, President Kennedy recognised these legitimate grievances and suggested ways of meeting them. To assist companies who face this situation, he suggested that governments should offer financial assistance to enable them to change to other products, special loans should be available at low rates of interest for new plant, and a remission of tax should be granted during the period of transition. To assist the workers also affected, President Kennedy thought that governments should offer special unemployment benefits, arrange special courses for re-training and assist workers who had to move to new homes. These plans were discussed seriously by United Nations Committees and by Western governments.

They must also become part of the policy of the E.E.C. if that organisation is to be 'outward looking', and thus able to play a full part in the 'War on Want'.

The problems posed by the growing gap between the rich and the poor in the world are as important and as dangerous as any which face us in the mid-twentieth century. Many of the facts have been given above, but three points need special emphasis:

1 Though much good may be done by local organisations in attempting to raise money for the relief of poverty, there can be little doubt that if this problem is ever to be solved, it will require action by governments acting together. In a democracy, the electorate should be given some idea of the attitude of the parties in this matter and should be informed of its true significance.

2 Financial aid and the development of trade depend to a great degree upon the economic health of the rich countries. A balance-of-payments crisis can reduce both aid and trade, as the United States discovered in 1960, and as Great Britain discovered in 1961. It seems likely, therefore, that no satisfactory long-term answer will be found in the West to this problem until the rich countries can rely upon full employment and permanent growth. For this, some form of wages-and-incomes policy seems essential, and possibly some form of international control over national currencies.

3 However much nations plan to give assistance to the underdeveloped countries, the basic problem is one of population control. The difficulties here are very great (*see page 217*) and, indeed, it may be that the newly independent peoples will need time to overcome their early nationalism before either the United Nations or the developed countries can expect any serious effort to be made to solve this incredibly complex problem. The question is whether the world has time to wait.

THE POST-WAR YEARS: A SUMMARY OF EVENTS

1945

February	Churchill, Roosevelt and Stalin sign the Yalta Agreement
March	The Berne negotiations
April	U.S. troops cross the Elbe—53 miles from Berlin Death of President Roosevelt. Mr Truman becomes President of the U.S.A. The San Francisco Conference: UNO is established
May	Germany surrenders
July	General election in Britain. Attlee succeeds Churchill as Prime Minister The Potsdam Conference
August	Japan surrenders
Aug.–Dec.	Communist governments established in Rumania, Bulgaria and Hungary

1946

April	Churchill's Fulton speech
May	Soviet troops finally withdrawn from Iran
October	Ships of British navy mined in Corfu Channel
December	Ho Chi Minh begins campaign against French in Indo-China

1947

January	United States and British zones of occupation in Germany are merged
February	The British withdraw from Greece
March	The 'Truman Doctrine'—aid to Greece and Turkey Treaty of Dunkirk (Britain and France)
June	Marshall Aid offered to Europe
August	Britain withdraws from India—followed by violence between Moslems and Hindus as transmigrations increase
September	U.N. Commission is refused entry into North Korea
October	Britain recognises Burma as an independent state The Cominform is established
November	The British government announces decision to withdraw from Palestine
December	Communist government is set up in Northern Greece

1948

February	Federation of Malaya established—followed by outbreak of rebellion
	Czechoslovakia becomes Communist
	Soviet-Finnish Treaty
	Western powers hold talks on future of Germany
March	Benelux Treaty signed in Brussels
May	Syngman Rhee elected President of South Korea
	State of Israel proclaimed—followed by start of Arab-Israeli War
June	Reform of currency in West Germany
	Berlin blockade
	U.S. aid promised to signatories of Brussels Treaty
	Airlift to Berlin begins
	Yugoslavia is expelled from Cominform
August	Partisans for Peace Organisation is set up in Poland
December	The Soviet Union completes evacuation of North Korea

1949

January	United Nations arrange cease-fire in Kashmir
February	Arab-Israeli armistice is signed in Rhodes
April	NATO established
	H.M.S. *Amethyst* is shelled in Yangtse River
	United States, British and French zones of occupation in Germany are merged
May	End of Berlin blockade
	German Federal Republic established
	Opening of new Foreign Ministers' Conference
June	U.S. evacuates South Korea
August	Dr Adenauer and Christian Democrats win election in West Germany
	Foreign Ministers of American States meet at Santiago
October	Communist government set up in Peking
	Herr Grotewohl becomes leader of People's Republic in East Germany
November	West Germany admitted to the Council of Europe
December	Chiang Kai-shek flees to Formosa

1950

February	Sino-Russian Treaty of Friendship
May	West Germany enters European Iron and Steel Community

June	North Korea attacks South Korea
July	Fifty nations promise assistance to the United Nations in Korea
September	Great Britain and the U.S.S.R. agree that Communist China should be represented in the United Nations
	Western Powers end state of war with Germany
October	European Defence Community (E.D.C.) first discussed
November	General MacArthur encounters Communist Chinese troops in Korea
	The Uniting for Peace Resolution is passed by the General Assembly of the United Nations
December	Mr Attlee, British Prime Minister, visits Washington

1951

February	United Nations condemns Communist China as an aggressor
April	General MacArthur is recalled to the U.S.A.
	In Korea, the front is stabilised along the 38th parallel
	Anglo-Iranian oil dispute begins with nationalisation of Anglo-Iranian Oil Co. by Dr Mussadiq
June	King Abdullah of Jordan is assassinated
September	Iranian troops seize Abadan Oil Refinery

1952

July	International Court at The Hague rules nationalisation of Anglo-Iranian Oil Company to have been a domestic issue
	Coup d'état in Egypt overthrows King Farouk
	General Neguib and Colonel Nasser assume command of the new Republic
October	General Templer (earlier appointed High Commissioner) reports military situation finally in hand in Malaya
November	General Eisenhower elected President of the U.S.A.

1953

March	Death of Stalin
May	Churchill suggests high-level Summit Meeting
June	Praesidium in Moscow votes (not unanimously) for the withdrawal of Soviet troops from East Germany
	East German rising
July	Armistice signed in Korea—at Panmunjon
August	Fall of Dr Mussadiq

1954

January	Berlin Conference—the Great Powers fail to reach a settlement on Germany
February	Turkey and Pakistan sign Defence Treaty
April–May	Geneva Conference
	Fall of Dien Bien Phu
July	Settlement in Indo-China—Vietnam, Laos and Cambodia became independent
August	Balkan Pact signed by Yugoslavia, Greece and Turkey
	E.D.C. not ratified by the French National Assembly
September	SEATO established
October	German Federal Republic joins NATO
	British troops withdraw from the Suez Canal Zone
November	F.L.N. begins rebellion in Algeria
December	End of Anglo-Iraqi Treaty

1955

March	W.E.U. ratified
April	Bandung Conference of Afro-Asian Countries
May	Occupation of Germany formally ended by Western Powers
	Warsaw Pact signed by powers of the Soviet bloc
July	Geneva Summit Meeting—Eisenhower's 'Open Skies' proposals rejected
	Mr Shepilov, Soviet Foreign Minister, makes first visit to Egypt
September	Colonel Nasser announces 'Arms Deal' with the Soviet Union
October	Baghdad Pact completed by the adherence of Iran

1956

February	Twentieth Soviet Communist Party Congress—Mr Khrushchev denounces Stalin and his policies
	M. Guy Mollet visits Algiers
April	Bulganin and Khrushchev visit Britain
May	Egypt recognises Communist China
June	Mr Shepilov, Soviet Foreign Minister, visits Cairo
July	Colonel Nasser meets Nehru and Tito at Brioni, Yugoslavia
	U.S. and British governments withdraw offers of financial help for the Aswan High Dam
	Egypt nationalises the Suez Canal Company

August	Twenty-four Nation Conference meets in London—formation of the Suez Canal Users Association (S.C.U.A.)
October	Imre Nagy becomes Prime Minister of Hungary, succeeding the Stalinist Rakosi Nationalist rising in Hungary Israeli invasion of Egypt Anglo-French ultimatum to Egypt and Israel
November	Anglo-French invasion of Port Said Nagy withdraws Hungary from Warsaw Pact Soviet tanks return to Budapest. Nagy Government overthrown. Janos Kadar appointed Prime Minister of Hungary British and French governments accept U.N. resolution calling for a cease-fire, and withdraw from Suez Canal on arrival of U.N. troops U.N. condemns U.S.S.R. for failing to withdraw from Hungary

1957

March	'Eisenhower Doctrine' promulgated Treaty of Rome signed by France, Italy, West Germany, Belgium, Netherlands and Luxembourg
April	Crisis in Jordan—U.S. 6th Fleet sails for Eastern Mediterranean
August	Crisis in Syria. President Eisenhower declares that Syria has fallen under Communist influence
September	Mr Loy Henderson, U.S. envoy to Turkey, refused permission to enter Syria
October	Publication of the Rapachi Plan for disengagement in Central Europe Herr Willy Brandt, leader of Social Democrats, becomes Mayor of West Berlin Sputnik I encircles the earth Mr Khrushchev claims knowledge of a U.S. plot to bring about Turkish invasion of Syria

1958

January	E.E.C. and Euratom established
February	Syria and Egypt unite to form U.A.R.—later joined by the Yemen Kings Feisal of Iraq and Hussein of Jordan form the Arab Federation
May	Rising in Algiers—General Massu proclaimed leader. Committee of Public Safety set up

June	General de Gaulle takes over the government of France after stating conditions for investiture
July	Nagy and Maleter executed King Feisal of Iraq, Crown Prince Ilahi and Prime Minister Nuri es Said are murdered in revolt led by General Kassim U.S. Marines land at Beirut in the Lebanon following constitutional crisis British paratroops land in Jordan
August	Singapore becomes a self-governing state
November	Berlin Crisis—Mr Khrushchev demands recognition for East Germany and withdrawal of Western powers from West Berlin

1959

January	Fidel Castro seizes power in Cuba General de Gaulle elected President of the Fifth French Republic
March	Iraq withdraws from the Baghdad Pact
May	Improvement in Anglo-Egyptian relations
September	Eisenhower-Khrushchev meeting at Camp David
December	Establishment of EFTA

1960

January	Following de Gaulle's dismissal of Massu, rising of extremists in Algiers led by Ortiz and Lagaillarde
March	Police fire on unarmed crowd of Negroes at Sharpeville, South Africa
April	First Aldermaston March in Great Britain (C.N.D.)
May	Flight of U.S. reconnaissance plane (the U2) over the U.S.S.R. Failure of the Summit Conference in Paris
August	de Gaulle offers independence to Middle Congo Belgium grants independence to the Congo
September	Disagreement between Congolese Nationalist leaders leads to civil war Conference of South American Republics at Bogota, Colombia
November	Mr John F. Kennedy elected President of the U.S.A.

1961

March	South Africa withdraws from the British Commonwealth
April	Revolt of Generals Challe, Zeller, Jouhaud and Salan in Algiers
June	Kennedy and Khrushchev meet in Vienna
July	Mass exodus from East Berlin
August	Berlin Crisis—the wall built across Berlin
	British Government applies to join the E.E.C. (Common Market)
	Inter-American Economic and Social Council at Punta del Este, Uruguay
	U.N. troops in the Congo ordered to seize mercenaries
September	War in Katanga between U.N. troops and Mr Tshombe's forces
	Russians resume nuclear tests and explode very powerful bombs
	Syria withdraws from the U.A.R.
	Mr Hammarskjoeld killed in plane crash at Ndola, Northern Rhodesia
November	Negotiations begin between Britain and the E.E.C.
December	General Assembly of the United Nations designate 1960's as 'Decade of Development'

1962

March	Settlement of the Franco-Algerian War
June	The O.A.S. sign truce with Algerian government
July	Agreement on Laos signed after neutralist Prince Souvanna Phouma becomes Prime Minister
August	Plan for peace in the Congo put forward by U Thant
September	Revolt in the Yemen—Imam forced to flee
	Ben Bella elected Prime Minister of Algeria
October	Discovery of Russian missile installations in Cuba—followed by the Cuban crisis
November	China attacks India
December	U.S.A. and Great Britain sign Nassau Agreement

1963

January	Death of Mr Gaitskell, leader of British Labour Party; succeeded by Mr Harold Wilson
	U.N. troops defeat Mr Tshombe's forces in Katanga
	President de Gaulle refuses Britain entry into E.E.C.
February	General Kassim murdered in Iraq

March	Colonel Aref forms a new government in Iraq
June	Intensification of Sino-Soviet quarrel
	Death of Pope John XXIII; succeeded by Pope Paul VI
	Establishment of a 'hot line' between U.S.S.R. and U.S.A., providing immediate communication between the two Heads of State
July	Partial Test Ban Treaty signed in Moscow
September	Federation of Malaysia established
October	Mr Harold Macmillan succeeded by Sir Alec Douglas Home as Prime Minister of Great Britain
	Dr Adenauer succeeded by Dr Erhard as Chancellor of West Germany
	Partial Test Ban Treaty becomes effective. France and China are not among the signatories
November	Mr Lyndon Johnson becomes President of the U.S.A. on assassination of President Kennedy
December	Outbreak of fighting between Greeks and Turks in Cyprus

1964

January	France recognises Communist China and President de Gaulle suggests neutralisation of South-east Asia
April	New state of Tanzania formed by the union of Tanganyika and Zanzibar
May	Death of Mr Nehru; succeeded as Prime Minister of India by Mr Lal Bahadur Shastri
September	Malta becomes independent and joins British Commonwealth
October	Sudden dismissal of Mr Khrushchev; succeeded as Premier of U.S.S.R. by Mr Alexei Kosygin
	Mr Leonid Brezhnev becomes First Secretary of the Communist Party
	In Great Britain, the Labour Party regains power after thirteen years in opposition; Mr Harold Wilson becomes Prime Minister
	Communist China explodes her first nuclear bomb
November	President Johnson defeats the Republican opponent, Senator Goldwater
	Cease-fire in the Yemen
	Belgian paratroops land in the Congo to protect Europeans

1965

January	Death of Sir Winston Churchill
February	Intensification of U.S. military effort in Vietnam; bombing of North Vietnam continues

April	Fighting breaks out between India and Pakistan in the Rann of Kutch
	U.S. marines land to stop fighting in Santo Domingo, capital of the Dominican Republic
May	EFTA Prime Ministers meeting in Vienna agree to closer links with E.E.C.
June	Commonwealth Prime Ministers' Conference in London; suggested Peace Mission to Vietnam
	In Algeria, President Ben Bella overthrown by Colonel Boumedienne
July	France quarrels with other E.E.C. members on agricultural policy
August	Singapore secedes from Federation of Malaysia
	Severe fighting between Indians and Pakistanis in Kashmir
	President Nasser talks with King Feisal of Saudi-Arabia. Egyptian troops to be withdrawn from Yemen
September	India and Pakistan agree to U.N. demand for a cease-fire; China withdraws her ultimatum to India
	In Germany, the Christian Democratic Party wins the West German elections; Dr Erhard remains Chancellor
	In Aden, constitution suspended following riots
November	Rhodesia makes a Unilateral Declaration of Independence

SOME ABBREVIATIONS

ANZUS	Australia, New Zealand, U.S.A.
BENELUX	Belgium, the Netherlands, Luxembourg
CENTO	Central Treaty Organisation (Baghdad Pact)
C.N.D.	Campaign for Nuclear Disarmament
COMECON	Council of Mutual Economic Aid
E.D.C.	European Defence Community
E.E.C.	European Economic Community
EFTA	European Free Trade Association
EURATOM	European Atomic Energy Community
F.A.O.	Food and Agriculture Organisation
F.L.N.	National Liberation Force (Algeria)
GATT	General Agreement on Tariffs and Trade
I.L.O.	International Labour Organisation
NATO	North Atlantic Treaty Organisation
O.A.S.	Secret Army Organisation (Algeria)
SEATO	South-East Asia Treaty Organisation
SHAPE	Supreme Headquarters Allied Power Europe
U.A.R.	United Arab Republic
UNESCO	United Nations Educational, Scientific and Cultural Organisation
UNCOK	United Nations Committee on Korea
UNO	United Nations Organisation
W.E.U.	Western European Union
W.H.O.	World Health Organisation

INDEX

SOME SUGGESTIONS FOR FURTHER READING

BAADE, F. The race to the year 2000

BOYD ORR, LORD, & TOWNSEND, P. What's happening in China

CAMERON, J. The African revolution

CHURCHILL, SIR W. S. The Second World War

FITZGERALD, C. P. Flood tide in China

GRIFFITHS, SIR P. Modern China

GUNTHER, J. Inside Europe today

LAQUEUR, W. Z. The Soviet Union and the Middle East

MASON, P. Year of decision

MAXWELL, R. (Ed.) War on want

MORRIS, J. The Hashemite kings

P.E.P. World population and resources

ROBERTSON, T. Crisis

SCHWARTZ, B. I. Chinese communism and the rise of Mao

TAYLOR, A. J. P. The origins of the Second World War

WILMOTT, C. The struggle for Europe

WOODHOUSE, C. M. British foreign policy since the Second World War

Printed in Great Britain by Ebenezer Baylis & Son Ltd.,
The Trinity Press, Worcester and London

VTT